GORP, GLOP & GLUE STEW

Favorite Foods from 165 Outdoor Experts

Yvonne Prater and
Ruth Dyar Mendenhall

Cartoons by Dale Martin

"Well, so much for the food."

THE MOUNTAINEERS/SEATTLE

THE MOUNTAINEERS: Organized in 1906
"...to explore, study, preserve, and enjoy
the natural beauty of the Northwest."

First printing December 1981, second printing June 1983,
third printing June 1984, fourth printing January 1986,
fifth printing April 1988, sixth printing March 1991

Published by The Mountaineers
1011 S.W. Klickitat Way, Suite 107, Seattle, WA 98134

Published simultaneously in Canada by Douglas & McIntyre, Ltd.
1615 Venables Street, Vancouver, British Columbia V5L 2H1

Published simultaneously in Great Britain by Cordee
3a DeMontfort St., Leicester, England LE1 7HD

Book design by Marge Mueller
Manufactured in the United States of America

Library of Congress Cataloging in Publication Data

Prater, Yvonne.
    Gorp, glop & glue stew.

    Includes index.
    1. Outdoor cookery. I. Mendenhall, Ruth.
II. Title. III. Title: Gorp, glop, and glue stew.
TX823.P69   641.5'78   81-18836
ISBN 0-89886-017-2   AACR2

CONTENTS

133 PART THREE: WILD FOOD FEASTING

159 PART FOUR: BETTER FOOD, LESS WORK

PREFACE

Backpackers, mountain climbers, cross-country skiers, snowshoers, dogsledders, canoeists, survival specialists, guides—all are practical and experienced camp cooks. These are the people who contributed the recipes for *Gorp, Glop & Glue Stew*.

Every recipe in the book is backed up by the addition of a short biography of the contributor and enlivened by anecdotes about haps and mishaps connected with food and other phases of outdoor life. Valuable tips for outdoor eating abound, and so do the special attractions of many far-flung places.

These outdoor cooks come from all over the United States, from Canada, and elsewhere. They have ranged across peaks and valleys, deserts and waterways, woodland, farmland, and wild land. They have lit one-burner stoves or old-time campfires (or subsisted on squirrel food) in the Rockies, the Sierra Nevada, the Cascades, the Wasatch Range, the Tetons, the Adirondacks, the Alps, and the Antarctic. They have camped on mountainsides in Alaska and Hawaii; on lakes, rivers, swamps, and seashores in the Midwest and the Southeast. They have cooked in Canada, Chile, and China; in Patagonia, Peru, and Pakistan. Their suggestions include meals for one-day walks; for weekend, week-long, or eight-month backpacks; and for long stays on glaciers, or in hammocks on Big Walls in the West.

Their camp kettles have received foods from supermarket and nettle beds, from mountaineering shops and mousetraps. Some cuisine reflects gourmet creativity; much shows practicality, or lack of interest in eating compared with other pursuits.

All the recipes in this book have been field-tested by real people, who also exude philosophies of cooking and eating in diverse place and circumstance. The accompanying anecdotes record the joys and jokes, the miseries and misfortunes, the personalities and camaraderie associated with outdoor travel, cooking, and eating. This is a cookbook, and also a book about the cooks.

Ruth Dyar Mendenhall

ACKNOWLEDGMENTS

Work on this book started four years ago. Since my husband, Gene Prater, is a well-traveled snowshoer and mountain climber, I picked his brain first for names to contact. Then I researched outdoor books and magazines. Each person I contacted seemed to lead me to others, in that loosely-linked chain of comradery that encompasses those active in the outdoors.

Since I'd selected backcountry-outdoor people who were literally "out" most of the time, my best results in contacting them were achieved via phone around Christmas and New Year's when hearth and home recalled the wanderers. In that two-to-four week session of calls lasting up to an hour apiece, my local long distance operators came to know my voice instantly and helped my search; my backside got numb; I developed an allergy to the plastic of the telephone; and I learned to take notes and recipe proportions *very* fast.

There was sometimes discomfort on the other end of the call, too. As my conversation with Fred Beckey neared the end, he said, "Well, I have to ring off now. It's raining here in California. My phone is located on a pole in the backyard and I'm getting drenched!"

My coauthor, Ruth Dyar Mendenhall, and I would like to express deep appreciation to the following for their help on this project: John Pollock, for first suggesting this outdoor cookbook and for his continuing interest and encouragement; Louise Marshall, for helping compose and follow up on the letter requesting the recipe-anecdote-nutshell biography that captured the essence of what we were after; Mountaineers Books staff members, Donna DeShazo, for her long involvement in the project, and Ann Cleeland, for her editorial supervision; Dale Martin, for his rib-tickling cartoons; Marge Mueller, for her book design and cartoon ideas; Molly Killingsworth, for copy editing; Pete Madeira of the Appalachian Mountain Club, Doris Herwig of the Adirondack Mountain Club, and Frank Ashley, who edits a western backpacking newsletter, for their assistance in locating contributors; and most of all, the contributors themselves, who really wrote the book. (Thanks also to those who responded whose recipes weren't included due to duplication or space limitations.)

Collecting this delightful, one-of-a-kind assortment of delicious food ideas and experiences has encouraged me, in planning a backcountry outing, to think like these interesting adventurers. May you likewise enjoy reading and employing their advice on food in the outdoors.

Yvonne Prater

Logan bread can be used in place of rocks for driving off bears.

PART ONE

Homemade Backpack Foods

Campers often wonder if there is a better way when their bread is squashed in the pack due to intimate contact with tent stakes; cookies turn to crumbs; candy seems to be composed of chemicals; jerky costs as much as gold. Similar and often superior foods that are nutritious, delicious, more economical, and often much more durable can be made at home. Such homemade specialties are generally easy to make and nearly always satisfactory.

Exact measurements are important in baked goods, though not critical or necessary in many types of recipes. All measurements in this part of the book are standard American cookbook measurements:

    1 cup = 8 fluid ounces
    1 teaspoon means a level teaspoonful
    1 tablespoon, also level = 3 teaspoons
    4 tablespoons = ¼ cup or 2 ounces

In some recipes, both the weight (in ounces or pounds) and the fluid measure are given for convenience.

Oven temperatures are given in degrees Fahrenheit.

Breads for the Pack

Victor Josendal and Keith Hart
ORIGINAL LOGAN BREAD

4 cups water
3½ to 4 pounds (13 to 16 cups) whole wheat flour
12 ounces (1½ cups) melted shortening
1 pound (1½ cups) honey
12 ounces (1½ cups) sugar
1 pound (2 cups) blackstrap molasses (optional)
4 ounces (1½ cups) dry milk (preferably whole dry milk)
1 teaspoon salt
2 teaspoons baking powder

Add all ingredients to the water, and mix thoroughly. Put into muffin tins; or run the dough into a pan till it is about ½ inch thick, and groove into 3-inch squares. Bake at 300° for 1 hour, or longer if a drier lighter-weight product is desired. Makes about 5 dozen muffin-sized bricks.

Victor (Vic) Josendal of Seattle, Washington has been credited with popularizing Logan Bread through his description in a 1953 Mountaineers newsletter. Vic started climbing in 1946 and has since made countless ascents in the Cascades, including the first ascent in 1958 of Mt. Fury. He was a member of the 1952 King Peak-Yukon expedition, was with the 1964 Cordillera Blanca Seattle group that climbed 22,205-foot Huascarán, and more recently was on a trip to Mt. Fairweather in Glacier Bay National Monument in Alaska.

❝ This special concentrated bread for climbers was first used by the 1950 Mt. Logan expedition from the University of Alaska. It proved to be wholesome and delicious, and has been a basic food on many expeditions to Alaska, Canada, and the Yukon. It also holds a strong place in memories of those who made long sojourns into the Cascades; it sometimes sustained life when other food ran out, and it stirred up both controversy and high praise. If dried out too much it becomes hard as concrete; various methods of rehydration include soaking it in tea, soup, or hot fruit-flavored gelatin. The recipe has survived many years of use, and seems to be here to stay—for better or worse. ❞

Keith Hart of Auk Bay, Alaska was on the first ascents of 17,130-foot King Peak in the St. Elias Range, and of 12,002-foot Mt. Drum and 15,030-foot

University Peak in the Wrangells. He has made many climbs elsewhere in Alaska, including winter ascents. Keith has worked as an avalanche specialist for various agencies in Alaska, and as a snow ranger with the U.S. Forest Service.

❝ This is the origin of Logan Bread—or as much of it as I know. In 1950, Gordon Herreid was the leader of the University of Alaska party to climb Mt. Logan (19,850 feet elevation in the southwest Yukon Territory of Canada). Herreid induced a now-forgotten baker in Fairbanks to make an indestructible high-energy 'bread' for the group. One of the other members of the Logan party, Alston (Al) Paige, was the leader of the 1952 University of Alaska climb of King Peak. It was Al who introduced me to Logan Bread. For a couple of years thereafter I was an advocate of The bread. The stuff was baked to the texture of charcoal briquets. We would tenderize the chunks with an ice axe, or by dunking in hot liquids. (Before tenderizing, they could be used in place of rocks for driving off bears.) Around 1956 or 1957, I had Logan Bread tested to determine its food value. I was somewhat shocked to find that nutritionally it equaled graham crackers. However, it retains superiority in durability, concentrated volume, and long 'shelf life.'

One of my food adventures occurred some years ago during a Christmas vacation. T. Neal Davis, another University of Alaska student, and I planned to ski the sixty miles from Nanana to Fairbanks, following the course of the frozen Tanana River. Shortly after starting, we found that the unseasonably warm temperature (about 10° F) had caused much of the river ice to be covered by a thin layer of frost crystals, with open water at intervals. The skiing was very rough, and after covering only about ten miles in several hours (mostly by the light of the moon and the aurora borealis), we saw the remains of a partially collapsed log cabin which offered some shelter. We started a campfire and scooped up snow to melt for dinner. When the melt water finally began to boil, and I was ready to add other ingredients, my flashlight revealed, bubbling in our water, numerous rabbit droppings which had been buried in the snow. Being a squeamish type, I pitched out the water and contents, and started over with new snow from the roof. Neal was dismayed that I hadn't just scooped out the foreign bodies and used the water. We still debate the proper method of coping with rabbit droppings in the dinner. ❞

Herb and Jan Conn
APPLE LOGAN BREAD

1½ cups water
1¾ cups sugar
2 cups applesauce
½ cup molasses
⅔ cup honey
2 cups shortening
7 to 8 cups (2 pounds) whole wheat flour

2⅔ cups white flour
⅔ cup dry milk
1 teaspoon baking powder
2 teaspoons baking soda
1 teaspoon salt
1 generous teaspoon ground cloves
1 generous teaspoon ground nutmeg

Mix water, sugar, applesauce, molasses, honey, and shortening. Bring mixture to the boiling point. Mix the dry ingredients together thoroughly, and add to the liquid mix. Pour dough into greased loaf pans, filling pans about ⅔ full. Bake at 300° for about 1 hour. Cool, remove from pans, wrap in foil, and store in refrigerator.

Herb and Jan Conn, who live near Custer, South Dakota are a husband and wife climbing and caving team of long standing. They were pioneer rock climbers in the Washington, D.C. area in the early 1940's. They have made various ascents in the Tetons and elsewhere. Herb was on the first ascent in 1949 of Agathlan in Monument Valley, Arizona and in 1950 was in a party that made a new route on Devils Tower, Wyoming.

Herb and Jan moved to the Needles area in the Black Hills of South Dakota in 1949. Between then and 1960 they put up 215 first ascents in this now popular climbing mecca. They also surveyed and mapped extensively in the region and over the years kept detailed records of climbing activities. Herb wrote the area's first climbing guide, a mimeographed treatise entitled "Rock Climbs in the Needles, Black Hills of South Dakota." The Conns' records and recollections were the basis of a 1971 guidebook written by Bob Kamps. Bob dedicated his book, *A Climber's Guide to the Needles in the Black Hills of South Dakota*, to Herb and Jan.

❝ We climbed—mostly in the Needles of the Black Hills—until we degenerated into cave exploring. The first cave we took a serious interest in was Jewel Cave (in Jewel Cave National Monument). We have spent almost twenty-two years trying without success to find the end of it, and we have mapped approximately sixty-six miles of underground passages. The cave continues to 'go' although we are slowing down a bit. Anyone curious to know more about the exploration and wonders of the cave should read *The Jewel Cave Adventure, Fifty Miles of Discovery Under South Dakota*, by Herb and Jan Conn. ❞

John E. Williamson
FRUIT-NUT LOGAN BREAD

2 cups honey
1 cup molasses
4 to 8 eggs
2 cups vegetable oil
15 cups flour (half white and half
   whole wheat; or cornmeal,
   cracked wheat, etc., in
   proportions to taste)

Dried fruit to taste (raisins, apricots,
   apples, etc.)
2 cups assorted nuts
2 cups sugar, brown or raw
2 teaspoons baking powder
2 teaspoons salt
2 cups dry milk

Mix honey, molasses, eggs, and oil together. In a second bowl, mix the dry ingredients. Combine wet and dry ingredients, and mix thoroughly. Form dough into 12 to 14 loaves. Bake for 2 to 3 hours at 150°.

John E. (Jed) Williamson, of Nottingham, New Hampshire, over a twenty-year period climbed in Canada, Alaska, Mexico, and Russia; has guided climbs in Grand Teton and Mount Rainier national parks; and has been an instructor and director with a national outdoor training school. He teaches in the Department of Education at the University of New Hampshire and is a recent director of the American Alpine Club. He is the American Alpine Club editor of *Accidents in North American Mountaineering*, published annually by the AAC and the Alpine Club of Canada in the interest of climbing safety. In the fall of 1980 Jed was a member of the American expedition to Gongga-Shan in China. Gongga is the 24,900-foot peak formerly known as Minya Konka. (It was first climbed in 1932 by Terris Moore and Richard Burdsall, supported by Arthur B. Emmons, III and Jack Young. For twenty-five years it remained the highest peak climbed by Americans.)

❝ I call my recipe 'Variations on a Theme.' The secret is to make the stuff as tough to chew as possible so people will have an easy time rationing themselves. How? Cook it s–l–o–w–l–y at a low heat. The result is low-rise, high-nutrition, tougher-than-nails-to-chew bread. I once made enough for six people for fifty days—more than a hundred pounds. We had been given 250 pounds of raisins. After the trip, I couldn't bear to look at the bread for a while—and I still eat raisins only when I am desperate. ❞

Darryl Lloyd
MT. ADAMS LOGAN BREAD

2 cups water	1 tablespoon salt
7 cups whole wheat flour (2 pounds)	1 cup honey
1⅔ cups brown sugar (¾ pound)	½ cup molasses
2¼ cups dry milk (6 ounces)	⅝ cup vegetable oil
1 tablespoon baking powder	¾ cup wheat germ

Mix all ingredients well. Turn into greased 10 × 14 inch roasting pan (or equivalent). Bake at 300° for a little over an hour (usually 1 hour and 10 minutes). When done, cut loaf into 20 squares. Air-dry squares for about 20 minutes or until they are semidry. Wrap each square in plastic wrap, then put into plastic bags closed with twist ties. This amount (approximately 5 pounds) is about right for 4 people on a 5-day trip, allowing a 4-ounce square per person per day. The bread is palatable, moist, and quite sweet, and remains fresh for 2 weeks or more even in hot weather. It does not fall apart under rough handling.

Darryl Lloyd of Glenwood, Washington is director of an organization that runs combined wilderness travel and mountain climbing outings. The trips provide instruction in wilderness navigation, basic snow and ice climbing techniques, group food preparation, and other outdoor skills. Darryl, an experienced climber, grew up on the southern Washington ranch that is headquarters for the enterprise.

❝ As my twin brother, Darvel, said when he was codirector of our business some years ago, we have to be careful with the menus on our outings for several reasons. We are catering to people from throughout North America with a great variety of tastes. Food must be appetizing and as varied as possible. Also we are cooking over stoves at timberline and above, so we must make meals simple to cook. Food must be nutritious, with about 4000 calories per person per day, and heavy in carbohydrates. It must also be lightweight. The total dry weight of our meals runs a little more than 1¾ pounds per person per day (7 ounces for breakfast, 13 to 14 ounces for lunch, and 8 ounces for dinner).

Breakfasts are usually a hot beverage and a hearty cereal with fruit. Lunches are the heavy items, like Logan Bread, cheese, and nuts, which are nibbled on throughout the day. Dinners consist of a hot drink, soup mix, a freeze-dried main course (usually improved by adding vegetables, margarine, and spices), and an instant pudding. Before the trip, all breakfasts and dinners are bagged and labeled, so there is a minimum of confusion in camp and exactly the right amount of food for the entire outing. ❞

Lawrence J. Burke, II
MOUNTAIN BROWN BREAD

1 teaspoon baking soda
1 teaspoon salt
1 cup cornmeal
1 cup rye or graham (finely milled
  whole wheat) flour

1 cup unbleached white, or whole
  wheat, flour
1 cup molasses
2 cups sour milk, buttermilk, or yogurt
1 cup raisins

Combine the dry ingredients in a large bowl, add the remaining ingredients, and mix. Pour dough into greased 2-pound coffee cans; fill them no more than ⅔ full. Cover cans tightly. Place on rack or trivet in a few inches of boiling water in a tightly covered pot. Steam for 5 hours in the oven or on top of the stove. Check water level occasionally, and carefully add a little if needed.

Larry Burke, II is editor-in-chief of *Mariah/Outside*, a wilderness adventure magazine published in Chicago, Illinois.

❝ *Mariah/Outside* is the culmination of my lifelong affinity for the wilderness. From the time I was eight, I spent four months each year living and riding in the mountains and deserts of the American West. I later searched for fresh ski slopes in the Sierra Nevada and the French Alps, and made expeditions through the Sahara, the Congo, and South America. At a camp stop in the Sahara, a group of Legionnaires and Taureg tribesmen beckoned to us to share their tea and what looked like alphabet soup. Later we learned that the 'African alphabet soup' we had enjoyed was made of camel's blood and intestines.

Mountain Brown Bread is good served with peanut butter, margarine, or Gtetost—a dense sweet Scandinavian goat's milk cheese. It is especially good with my Wilderness Bread Spread, which can be made as follows: Core and peel a few pounds of firm, tart apples. Slice and put them in a large kettle with 1 to 2 cups orange juice. Simmer, adding cinnamon, cloves, nutmeg, and lemon juice to taste. Also add any desired combination of molasses, honey, brown sugar, and concentrated orange juice, in amounts desired. Stirring occasionally, simmer for 30 to 45 minutes, or until the consistency seems proper for a spread. You can also add raisins, dried apricots, and prunes, which have been soaked overnight in wine, rum, brandy (or even water). For a backpacking trip, pour the spread into tubes—or if it is too chunky, into a wider-mouthed container. ❞

John Fischer
LEAD BREAD

2 cups water
4 cups flour (a mixture of rye, whole wheat, etc., to taste)
½ to 1 teaspoon salt
2 cups dried fruit and nuts (dates, figs, pitted prunes, apples, broken cashews, etc.,
    in proportions to taste)

Mix all ingredients. Spread dough about 2 inches thick in a lightly oiled pan, or form into a flat lump. Bake at 200° for about 3 hours, with oven door slightly ajar. The bread is done when the moisture is gone and the loaf sounds hollow when you thump it. Amounts given in the recipe can be varied to make more or less, depending on need.

John Fischer of Bishop, California has made ascents in mountain ranges throughout the western United States and Canada, climbed the Mexican volcanoes, been on expeditions to Mt. McKinley and Mt. Logan, and made Big Wall climbs in Yosemite and in the Andes. He is director of a mountaineering school in the Palisades area of the Sierra Nevada, with headquarters in Bishop.

❝ We ate Lead Bread during our twenty-one day trip up 22,834-foot Aconcagua in Argentina. But it had taken a whole day to find a baker who would make it in expedition quantity. This brick-like loaf is a mutation of the famed Logan Bread. Due to its consistency and simple ingredients, it will keep indefinitely and survive the most rigorous transport (even airdrops) as long as it remains dry. You can really depend on its not going bad or turning to crumbs. Many is the time my mates and I have divvied up the day's portion with an ice axe. If you manage to slice it thin enough, it is almost like whole grain rye crackers, and it's good served with jam and butter. It can be moistened by immersion in soup or other liquids. Once at Kluane Lake, we let it sit out in the rain to reduce it to an edible sogginess. ❞

"I wondered why my wife called it lead bread!"

Sam Curtis
WHOLE WHEAT BACKPACKING BREAD

1 tablespoon dry yeast
1 tablespoon brown sugar
¼ cup lukewarm water
5 cups whole wheat flour
½ cup dry milk

2 cups warm water
1 tablespoon salt
3 tablespoons bacon fat or other
     shortening
6 tablespoons honey

Dissolve yeast and brown sugar in ¼ cup lukewarm water. Mix the flour and dry milk together. Mix the 2 cups of water, salt, shortening, and honey. Now combine the yeast and flour mixtures. Add the liquids, and stir well. Put the dough into 2 greased bread pans (about 8½ × 4½ × 2½ inches). Let rise in a warm place for 1 hour. Bake at 400° for about 45 minutes.

Sam Curtis of Bozeman, Montana is a licensed guide and an outdoor writer and photographer. He has hiked extensively in the United States, Canada, and Europe. He leads mountain, desert, and cold-weather trips that focus on camping skills and appreciation of the environment. Sam is author of *Harsh Weather Camping* and a contributor to such magazines as *Adventure Travel* and *Backpacker*.

❝ One of the most leisurely camp meals I've ever had was in a snow cave at 10,500 feet on the side of Mt. Cowan in the Montana Rockies. There were five of us. We had spent a lot of time slogging along on skis and shoveling snow before we could crawl into our makeshift home. Darkness slammed down by 5 p.m., leaving three or four hours before we would feel ready for the sack. Our multi-course meal, however, depended on melted snow as a basic ingredient, so we spent a good deal of that time sitting around the sputtering stove, mulling over the day's progress, and speculating on the possibility of reaching the summit next morning.

Cups of pea soup slowly gave way to 'cheese mac,' which faded into rehydrated meat bars, which lingered into copious cups of extra-thick hot chocolate. It was a repast of three hours in the cooking and eating—a very civilized meal in companionable surroundings, and an excellent way to pass the dark evening.

We didn't make it to the summit of Mt. Cowan the next day. A foot of new snow sealed over the snow cave during the night. This persuaded us not to dig out till oxygen seemed in short supply. We managed to ski down the glacial cirque without starting an avalanche and were thankful for that. ❞

Ruth Ittner
APRICOT-NUT LOAF

1 cup finely chopped dried apricots
1 cup warm water
2 cups flour (various whole grain and
nut flours may be combined to
taste; one good combination is
equal parts whole wheat, millet,
sesame, and sunflower)

¼ cup dry milk
2 teaspoons baking powder
1 teaspoon salt
¼ cup safflower oil
1 egg, beaten
¼ cup orange juice
1 cup walnuts, chopped

Soak apricots in warm water for 15 minutes. Drain, saving ¼ cup of the liquid. In a large bowl combine flours, dry milk, baking powder, and salt. In another bowl combine oil, egg, reserved apricot liquid, and orange juice. Add this mixture, plus the drained apricots and the walnuts, to the flour mixture. Stir just enough to moisten the dry ingredients. Spread in greased and floured 9 × 5 inch loaf pan. Bake at 350° for about 55 minutes, or until a toothpick inserted in the center comes out clean. Cool in pan for 10 minutes. Remove loaf from pan and finish cooling it on a wire rack; then refrigerate until used.

Ruth Ittner of Seattle, Washington hikes, backpacks, skis, and snow-shoes. She has also climbed in the North Cascades. Ruth is a research consultant with Institute of Governmental Research at the University of Washington.

❝ Like all outdoor people, I appreciate suitable trail food and consider this bread a real delicacy. I often use it for sandwiches, and it makes excellent snacks.

One of my favorite dehydrated dinners is one that I prepare myself at home before outings. It includes home-dried cooked hamburger, zucchini, tomatoes, and onions — in any proportions you prefer. Serve it with grated parmesan cheese. ❞

Anne LaBastille
QUICK HEALTH BREAD

2½ cups whole wheat flour
½ teaspoon cinnamon
¼ teaspoon salt
1 teaspoon baking soda
1 egg
½ cup molasses

¼ cup dark brown sugar, or honey
¼ cup safflower oil
⅔ cup buttermilk or yogurt
Grated orange or lemon peel, citron,
   dates, raisins, or nuts (to taste)

Mix flour, cinnamon, salt, and soda. Add the remaining ingredients, and mix. Pour into greased loaf pan (about 8½ × 4½ × 2½ inches) and bake about 50 minutes at 375°. Test for doneness with toothpick or pine needle. Cool the loaf. Eat, or wrap and store.

Anne LaBastille of New York State is one of the most experienced outdoorswomen in the eastern United States. Author, biologist, conservationist, and explorer, she has hiked and camped in the Adirondacks for more than fifteen years and is the only active woman registered guide in the state. She took her Ph.D. in wildlife ecology at Cornell University. Research and outdoor interests have taken her to Central America, the Caribbean Islands, the Amazon basin, and Europe. Numerous periodicals have published her popular and scientific articles.

Some years ago Anne acquired twenty-two acres on the shore of a lake in New York's six-million-acre Adirondack State Park—the largest wilderness area east of the Mississippi. In her book *Woodswoman*, she describes her experiences in building a small log cabin-studio which can be reached only by foot, boat, canoe, or snowmobile; there she splits her own wood and in winter chops a hole in the lake ice to get water. In her latest book, *Women and Wilderness*, she profiles fifteen other women who work and live in similar conditions. In *Assignment: Wildlife*, she describes her work with wildlife in tropical countries, where she often consults and where she has found that bread holds up well even without refrigeration.

❝ I like to carry a heavy, wholesome, sweet health bread. It goes well alone, or with cheese, peanut butter, and jelly. I first learned to depend on bread when hiking with European students in the Black Forest of Germany. Bread was the mainstay of most meals, with soup, cheese, sausages, and tea. ❞

Paul Ross
MONKEY BREAD

2 *eggs*	2 *cups flour*
⅔ *cup sugar*	½ *teaspoon salt*
⅓ *cup vegetable oil*	½ *teaspoon baking soda*
¼ *cup buttermilk*	½ *teaspoon baking powder*
1½ *large bananas, smashed*	½ *cup slivered almonds*

Mix eggs, sugar, and oil together. Add buttermilk and bananas. To this combination add the flour, salt, soda, and baking powder. Last, mix in the almonds. Put in a greased loaf pan and bake at 350° for about 50 minutes. To store, wrap in foil and put in refrigerator to keep it moist for climbs.

Paul Ross is a native of Britain who for some years has operated a climbing shop and mountaineering school at North Conway in the White Mountains of New Hampshire. He has done the Salathe Wall on El Capitan in Yosemite and has pioneered many routes in New England and Quebec. He is coauthor of *Rock Climber's Guide to the White Mountains.* He has made over a hundred new routes in the Lake District in England. He also made an early ascent of the Grand Capucin East and the first British ascent of the Bonatti Pillar of the Dru in the French Alps.

❞ In 1958 Don Whillans and I arrived in Chamonix to try the Bonatti Pillar. We were stuck in the valley for a week, due to bad weather. At last we set off with enormous packs for what was then considered the most technically difficult climb in the Western Alps. After the previous week's fast, we took five large loaves of bread, tubes of condensed milk, bacon, candies, chocolate, powdered soup, jam, sausage, and of course tea without which no British climber can face hard times. At the foot of the 3000-foot face, we met two other British climbers, Chris Bonington and Hamish MacInnes, and two Austrians.

We climbed all the next day and bivouacked on a good-sized ledge. At dark a rock the size of an orange struck MacInnes on the head (resulting in a skull fracture, we found out later). The next day, rockfall below intensified so we continued upwards. To move faster, we had to lighten our loads. I threw half our food down the face, and Whillans threw the other half. Our situation looked serious—but we still had one small packet of powdered soup, two 6 × 6 inch blocks of solid oatmeal, some hard candies, and a little tea. We knew we could not use the soup or tea till the top, as there was no water on the face. It took two more days to reach the summit, and another to descend in storm. All in all, it was an epic climb. But is an inch cube of oatmeal and two hard candies a day enough for such epics? ❞

Norman Wilson
DONNER SUMMIT BRAN BREAD

½ cup molasses	1 ½ cups flour
1 teaspoon baking soda	Dash salt
1 ½ cups buttermilk	Raisins, dates, sunflower seeds,
1 ½ cups bran	chopped nuts (to taste)

Combine molasses and baking soda. Add buttermilk and dry ingredients, and mix well. Add fruits, seeds, and/or nuts. Pour into oiled loaf pan. Bake at 350° for about 45 minutes, or until a toothpick or straw inserted into the loaf comes out clean.

Norman Wilson of Donner Summit, California has been involved in snow avalanche work for nearly thirty years. He has helped solve avalanche problems for ski areas, highway departments, land developments, and mining companies throughout the western United States, at Tuckerman Ravine in New Hampshire, and in Canada and Chile. He is a snow problems consultant and principal instructor for Canadian and American national avalanches schools, and is affiliated with the American Avalanche Institute of Wyoming and Colorado. An article by Norman on avalanche safety and route finding in avalanche terrain appeared in a 1977 *Mariah/Outside* magazine. Norman conducts four-day seminars in the Donner Summit area of the Sierra Nevada.

❝ We prepare students for recognition and avoidance of avalanche hazards, and give training in route finding and travel under avalanche conditions, and in backcountry avalanche rescues. About 80 percent of the instruction is in the field. We welcome stormy weather, which is frequent at 7000-foot Donner Summit where as much as 450 inches of snow may fall annually, and active avalanche slopes are numerous. Students come to our February-March seminars prepared for foul weather and willing to stay out all day. They must be in good physical condition and able to ski uphill and down on changeable terrain in varying snow conditions. Besides proper clothing and ski equipment, students bring a ten- to twenty-power hand lens to examine snow crystals.

I live on old old Highway 40, which isn't plowed in winter. I ski a mile and a half between the plowed highway and my home. ❞

Bars, Cookies and Cakes
to Carry

"Gee, I'm sorry. At the time Fudgcicles seemed like such a good idea."

Harriett Barker
PEANUT BUTTER COOKIES

1 ½ cups chunky peanut butter
1 cup sugar
Unbeaten whites of 2 eggs

Combine ingredients. Drop by teaspoonfuls onto an ungreased cookie sheet. Bake at 350° for 10 minutes; or bake in camp in a reflector oven till done. To prevent crumbling, cool in the pan for a few minutes.

Harriett Barker, who for some years taught a course on "Preparing Your Own Wilderness Food" at a California college, grew up in Washington State, where she was introduced to the outdoors by her parents. She now lives in Meadview, Arizona with her husband, Hal. The couple has canoed and backpacked in many parts of the West. Harriett is the author of *The One Burner Gourmet* and *Supermarket Backpacker* and is a member of OWAA (Outdoor Writers' Association of America).

❝ One lesson learned from experience is to label your food packages. On a 400-mile canoe trip down the Pelly and Yukon rivers to Dawson, several groups were fixing breakfast along the shore. I had planned pancakes with syrup for Hal and me. To make the syrup, I put what I thought was light brown sugar, with some water, on to boil. I stirred and stirred, but the mixture remained murky. I finally smelled it and found that I had used an unlabeled package of instant butterscotch pudding, that evening's dessert.

I have checked out and tested many packaged foods from supermarkets. We have lived exclusively on such foods for a month by supplementing them with home-dried fruits and vegetables. I had a home drier built, but found out that one of the fastest ways to dry food is to spread it on a fiberglass screen tray and put it inside a black car (with the windows almost closed) on a blacktop parking lot on a sunny day. I have dried peppers, celery, and mushrooms in half a day by this system. ❞

Arlene Blum
ANNAPURNA ENERGY BARS

Graham cracker crust (mix or from scratch)
8 ounces shredded coconut
18-ounce package chocolate or carob chips or morsels
18-ounce package butterscotch chips or morsels
½ cup walnuts
1 14-ounce can sweetened condensed milk

Line a 9-inch square pan with graham cracker crust. Mix the coconut, chocolate and butterscotch chips, and nut meats, and spread into the crust. Cover with condensed milk. Bake at 350° for 30 minutes. Cool. Cut into squares and wrap each square.

Arlene Blum was leader of the first all-woman American expedition to attempt an 8000-meter (26,000-foot) Himalayan peak. Under her leadership, the 1978 American Women's Himalayan Expedition put two women, Vera Komarkova and Irene Miller (now Irene Beardsley), and two Nepalese Sherpas on top of 26,545-foot Annapurna I by the Dutch Rib. The story of the climb is told in Arlene's book, *Annapurna: A Woman's Place*.

Arlene, a biochemist at the University of California at Berkeley, has a long record of climbs and treks in North and South America, Asia, and Africa. She was leader of the first ascent of Bhrigupanth (22,300 feet) by the 1980 Indo-American Women's Expedition to the Gangotri Glacier; deputy leader of the first all-woman ascent of Mt. McKinley in 1970; and a member of the American Bicentennial Everest Expedition in 1976. Among her ascents are Mt. Waddington in British Columbia; Ras Dashan, 15,158 feet, Ethiopia's highest peak; five summits of the Ruwenzori group in Uganda; Mt. Kenya, 17,058 feet, in Kenya; Kilimanjaro, 19,340 feet, in Tanzania; and high peaks in Afghanistan and India. She has also made a tour of the Elburz Mountains of northern Iran and climbed in the Pamir Range in Russia.

❝How do women keep in condition for Himalayan climbing? Some climb. Some spend a lot of time in such sports as soccer. I also enjoy long distance running and cross-country skiing.❞

Daniel Doan
MINCEMEAT COOKIES

1 9-ounce package condensed mincemeat
¾ cup water
2 cups graham cracker crumbs
1 14-ounce can sweetened condensed milk

Crumble mincemeat into a small saucepan, and add water. Cook and stir over medium heat until lumps are thoroughly broken up. Boil for 1 minute. Cool in large bowl. Add graham cracker crumbs and condensed milk, and mix well. Turn into greased 13 × 9 inch baking pan. Bake at 350° for 30 minutes, or until lightly browned. Cool in pan before cutting into squares. Store, and if possible carry, in rigid plastic container.

Daniel Doan of Sanbornton, New Hampshire started hiking in 1924. Ever since, he has been exploring New Hampshire's mountain ranges on foot. His books, *Fifty Hikes in New Hampshire's White Mountains* and *Fifty More Hikes in New Hampshire*, detail short walks, day hikes, and week-long backpacks. Included is New England's highest peak, 6288-foot Mt. Washington, which is noted for its changeable weather and record-breaking winds. Daniel not only backpacks year round, but also enjoys climbing, cross-country skiing, and snowshoeing.

❛❛ A few years ago I climbed Mt. Lafayette with friends and met a young man and a girl who were flying a red plastic kite from the summit. It looked like great fun! I have since occasionally carried a kite for the same purpose. Recently I flew one off the forehead of the Old Man of the Mountain, New Hampshire's famous granite profile on the side of Cannon Mountain.

Among good backpacking foods, lentils rank high. They should be presoaked (in a water bottle on the trail, or in a pot in camp). Season with instant minced onion, parsley flakes, celery seed, basil, thyme, and salt, and boil for about an hour. A cup of lentil soup made with stock rates 250 calories; the addition of tinned ham or similar meat brings it nearer 300. Historically, lentil soup is very ancient—lentils were used in Biblical times, and doubtless before that. The 'mess of pottage' for which Esau sold his birthright is said to have been of lentils. ❜❜

Gary Kuiper
DESERT NO-BAKE DROP COOKIES

1 cup sugar
½ stick (⅛ pound) butter or
  margarine
¼ teaspoon vanilla
2 tablespoons unsweetened cocoa

¼ cup peanut butter
¼ cup milk
½ cup uncooked quick oatmeal and/or
  nuts and coconut to taste

Mix sugar, shortening, vanilla, cocoa, peanut butter, and milk together in saucepan. Stir constantly while bringing mixture to a quick boil. Boil and stir for 3 minutes. Remove from heat. Add oatmeal and/or nutmeats and coconut. Drop by spoonfuls on waxed paper, and let stand awhile to cool and stiffen. Wrap.

Gary Kuiper started his outdoor career fighting forest fires in Montana and elsewhere in the West. Later he worked as a ranger for the National Park Service in Mississippi and Virginia. Transferred to the North Cascades National Park in Washington, he started backpacking to remote alpine areas. He is now chief ranger of Grand Canyon National Park in Arizona and makes backcountry trips in desert areas.

❝ Hiking in the desert requires specialized knowledge and equipment. Many of the 25,000 to 30,000 people who drive to the Grand Canyon on a typical summer day do not understand this. The South Rim, where my office is located, is at 7000 feet elevation, the North Rim at 9000 feet. Hikes here start downhill, an easy beginning. But the canyon is a mile deep; the bottom is reached by trails six to sixteen miles long; summer temperatures are usually in the 100s and may exceed 115 degrees; and coming back up is very demanding.

Under present regulations, we can check the equipment of overnight campers, who must apply for a camping permit; but we have no way of finding out ahead of time if day hikers are prepared for the conditions that exist. Some start down wearing only thongs, or even barefoot, with no sun protection or first-aid supplies. Most don't realize the importance of having water along—each person may require up to two gallons a day. Hikers often arrive at the canyon floor exhausted, dehydrated, and in need of help. The Park staff includes trained paramedics and emergency medical technicians who can determine whether such hikers can get back to the rim under their own power, with only a pep talk or with rest, liquid, and food, or whether they require mule or helicopter rescue (for which the rescued must pay). Most of our visitors enjoy the scenery and have a good time. But about 200 a year get into serious trouble—two young people died recently from severe dehydration. I wish more of our tourists were aware of the special rigors of desert trails. ❞

Richard J. Tucker
OLDE ENGLISH PLUM PUDDING

1-pound loaf white bread
Water to cover bread
1 pound seeded muscat raisins
1 pound seedless raisins
1 pound currants
⅛ pound candied citron, cut small
1 orange (grated rind and juice)
1 lemon (grated rind and juice)
½ cup sugar
½ pound white kidney suet, chopped fine or ground (get suet from butcher)

½ cup all-purpose flour
1 teaspoon cinnamon
½ teaspoon allspice
½ teaspoon salt
Eggs, 2 for each bowl used for steaming pudding
Baking powder, 2 teaspoons per bowl used for steaming pudding

Soak loaf of bread in water overnight. Squeeze out excess water, and beat bread till light with electric mixer or mixing spoon. Combine the bread, fruits, sugar, suet, flour, spices, and salt. Grease 6-inch diameter bowls well, and fill each about ⅔ full of batter. To each bowl add 2 eggs and 2 teaspoons baking powder, and mix thoroughly into batter in the bowl. Cover each bowl with cheesecloth tied tightly over the top with a string. In large kettle or kettles that can be tightly covered, set bowls of batter on rack in boiling water that comes about halfway up the bowls. Cover kettles, and steam puddings for 5 or 6 hours. Maintain water level by carefully adding more boiling water as necessary.

The finished puddings can be cut up and eaten as snacks or desserts. The pudding tastes best reheated and is very good served with hard sauce (a blend of powdered sugar, butter, and a dash of salt, with a flavoring such as vanilla, rum, etc.). People have been known to backpack in a little brandy, which can be poured over the pudding, lighted, and served flaming on a cold night.

Richard J. Tucker is a partner in a mountaineering equipment company in Waltham, Massachusetts.

❝ I have been climbing and backpacking since the late 1960's, mostly in New England in all seasons. I have also taken trips in the Colorado Rockies, the Tetons and Wind Rivers in Wyoming, the Cascades of Washington, Glacier National Park in Montana, the San Francisco Peaks and Grand Canyon areas of Arizona, and the Canadian Rockies, the Alps, and the Andes. I am a member of the National Ski Patrol and participate in kayaking, white-water canoeing, and long-distance ocean races. For lunches and snacks I like breads that are dense, moist, high in nutrition, and not easily crushed. The ultimate in calories and nutrition seems to be found in my great grandmother's plum pudding recipe—it is very complicated, but I think worth the effort. If properly made, the pudding keeps indefinitely without refrigeration. ❞

"Oh, aren't they adorable!"

David Mahre
HIGH-ENERGY FRUIT BARS

¼ pound (½ cup) butter or margarine
4 medium eggs, well beaten
1 cup sifted flour
½ teaspoon baking powder
1 teaspoon salt

1¾ cups sugar
2 cups dates, pitted and chopped
2 cups glazed (or candied) fruit
2½ cups chopped walnuts

Melt shortening and cool slightly. Add to well-beaten eggs. Sift together flour, baking powder, salt, and sugar, and add to the egg/shortening mixture. Mix fruits and nuts together, and combine with batter. Spread in 2 greased 9-inch square baking pans. Bake 30 minutes at 350°. Cool, cut into bars, and wrap individually in plastic wrap.

David Mahre and his wife, Mary, live at the White Pass ski area southeast of Mount Rainier National Park. David is manager of the ski area, and Mary is "mayor" of White Pass. All of their nine children ski. Twins Phil and Steve Mahre took part in the 1980 Winter Olympics at Lake Placid, where Phil won a silver medal; and in the 1981 World Cup ski races in Laax, Switzerland, where Phil became the first American to win the World Championship. Dave has climbed for many years. He put up new routes on the north sides of Stuart, Adams, Little Tahoma, and Rainier—particularly the Willis Wall area of Rainier. Due to frequent rockfall in some of these areas, Dave and his climbing friends took to wearing construction hard hats; they may have been the first in the United States to adopt such protection for climbing. Dave continues to climb, ski, and guide occasional parties.

❝ Most of my climbs have been done by small parties of no more than four or six. But some of my most memorable experiences were in assisting in the mass climbs of Mt. Adams that the Yakima Chamber of Commerce sponsored for eleven years. More than 400 people, many of them inexperienced, would gather and try to reach the top of the 12,276-foot volcanic cone.

A staff of fifty or more experienced climbers spent a week preparing the route for the mass ascent, and then took part in the climb itself. For me the affair became a highlight of the season. It was in part a reunion with climbers I had known for fifteen or twenty years but seldom saw.

As to food, I always relied on my buddies or my wife, Mary, to feed me. Mary often includes High-Energy Fruit Bars in my food supply, especially when I am called out unexpectedly on mountain rescues. I have traditionally provided T-bone steaks to grill on sticks for the first night out (when an open fire is possible). By the time the steaks fall into the fire a few times, swell up on the sticks, and are well charcoal-forged, they are ready to eat. No wonder my buddies were willing to do the cooking. ❞

Ralph Uber
PEAK PEPPERNUTS

2 cups sugar
2 cups dark corn syrup
1 cup butter or vegetable shortening
½ cup sour cream
1 teaspoon baking soda
11 cups flour (approximately; use
    enough to make a stiff dough)
1 teaspoon ginger

1 teaspoon allspice
1 teaspoon ground cloves
1 teaspoon ground nutmeg
2 teaspoons cinnamon
1 teaspoon salt
3 teaspoons baking powder
1 teaspoon crushed anise seeds
1 teaspoon cardamom seeds

Cream the sugar, syrup, and shortening together. Stir the soda into the sour cream, and add to the creamed mixture. Sift the flour, spices, salt, and baking powder together. Add anise and cardamom seeds. Mix the dry ingredients with the creamed mixture to form a stiff dough. Cut dough into small pieces and roll into balls. Place balls on greased cookie sheets, and bake at 325° for 15 minutes. Makes approximately 4 quarts.

Ralph Uber, M.D., a longtime resident of Yakima, Washington has made many climbs in the Cascades. In the early 1960's, his various ascents included two new routes on the west side of Mt. Adams, the second highest peak in Washington.

❝I once had a harrowing experience on Adams. I was climbing the icefall with Bob Swenson. The ice was exceptionally hard, and I was on a lead above Bob when I slipped. The only thing that saved me from severe injury or death was Bob's quick observation and action. He was able to jab his ice axe point a quarter-inch into the ice and hold me with his belay.❞

Rod Jeske
SWEETHEART LAKE CAKE

*8 ounces dried fruits (mixed; or any
    combination of apricots, peaches,
    raisins, dates, pears, etc.)*
¾ cup honey
2 tablespoons molasses
¼ pound (½ cup) butter

1 teaspoon baking soda
2 eggs, beaten
1 teaspoon dry yeast
1 cup granola
¾ cup sesame seeds
2 cups flour

*Cut dried fruit into small pieces, and put in saucepan. Soak fruit for 1 hour in just
enough water to cover it. Do not drain. Add honey, molasses, butter, and soda to
fruit. Simmer for 15 minutes. Cool to lukewarm. Add eggs and yeast. In a bowl mix
granola, sesame seeds, and flour. Pour the fruit mixture over the dry ingredients,
and mix well. Pour batter into a well-greased 8-inch square cake pan, and let rise in a
warm place for about 40 minutes. In an oven preheated to about 310°, bake for 2 hours
or a little longer. Cool before packing.*

Rod Jeske of Ellensburg, Washington is a mountaineer whose climbs and
excursions in the Cascades helped him decide on a career as a geologist. He
spent three years climbing and doing geological work in Alaska, where, in
an oven over a camp stove, he first baked his cake.

❝ A stand-out experience was a snowshoe trip I made in winter with
Joel Yelland and Jack Powell when we were Ellensburg college students. We
crossed the Cascades, going east from Darrington to Holden Village on Lake
Chelan. We started in a pouring rain, hiked up the road after dark, and
camped under a bridge—on the edge of a 100-foot drop-off, as we found out
when it got light. That day we hiked eighteen miles in slush to the end of the
road and put up our tent in the parking lot. The next day we continued
uptrail to near Cloudy Pass, where we found shelter in an old miner's cabin.
We crossed Cloudy Pass in such a thick whiteout that we couldn't tell up
from down. But we reached the Lyman Lake cabin safely and dried out
around a roaring wood stove. It was cozy, but the chimney didn't work so
the cabin was filled with smoke.
Next morning we headed down toward Holden in a snowstorm, with
avalanches rumbling above us in the fog. It was the hardest snowshoeing I
have ever done. The snow was twelve feet deep at Lyman Lake and so soft
we were sinking in waist deep at times. Trading the lead often, we kept on all
day and for an hour after dark. The lights of Holden Village were the most
welcome sight of my life. We were the first known snowshoers to make that
particular North Cascades crossing in winter. ❞

Steven and Anne Schneider
MOUNTAIN MANDELBRODT

1 cup sugar	4½ cups unbleached presifted flour
4 large eggs	(don't resift)
⅔ cup vegetable shortening	4 teaspoons baking powder
1¾ cups seedless raisins or currants	1 pinch salt
2 cups chopped walnuts	¼ cup sugar
⅓ cup each orange and lemon juice	1 teaspoon cinnamon
¼ teaspoon vanilla	

Put sugar and 2 of the eggs into electric blender. Blend at medium speed for 2 minutes till almost smooth. Add remaining eggs, and shortening. Blend at high speed till smooth, 1½ to 2 minutes. Pour this batter into large bowl. Add raisins and stir by hand till batter coats raisins. Add nuts and stir till coated. Add fruit juices and vanilla. Stir in 2 cups of the flour by hand. Add remaining flour, baking powder, and salt. Stir vigorously for 4 or 5 minutes till well blended—the dough is thick and heavy, and requires climber's muscles to mix. Refrigerate dough for 15 minutes.

With lightly floured hands, lift out pieces of dough about the size of small baked potatoes, form them into thick sausage shapes, and flatten slightly. Place (well spaced) on 2 greased cookie sheets. Combine the ¼ cup sugar with cinnamon, and sprinkle generously over flattened tops. Bake at 325° until evenly browned—watch closely after the first 30 to 35 minutes. Mandelbrodt is ready to eat when cool, but should be aged for 2 or 3 days before being taken on a trip.

Steven and Anne Schneider, a brother-sister climbing team from New Hampshire, operate a climbing school and guide service based in Hanover. They have written two books, *The Climber's Sourcebook* and *Backpacking on a Budget,* and Anne's backpacking articles have appeared in various periodicals. Anne has backpacked from Switzerland to northern Greece. Steve has climbed extensively in New England.

❝ Mandelbrodt is found in most Slavic countries, and probably in Austria and Germany. Some cooks use only raisins, some only nuts, and some add chocolate. Any way you make it, it's wonderful Big Wall food. A few winters ago a friend and I were climbing the 600-foot icicle on the Black Dike of Cannon Cliff and took a break to eat. At 20 below, the Mandelbrodt was frozen—those wonderful icy chunks kept us going. ❞

Laura and Guy Waterman
WINTER FRUITCAKE

3 ½ pounds mixed dried fruit
3 pounds raisins
16 cups cider (1 gallon)
8 cups whole wheat flour
7 cups rye flour
6 tablespoons grated orange rind

6 teaspoons ground cloves
12 teaspoons cinnamon
2 to 3 teaspoons ginger
2 teaspoons salt
5 cups almonds, blanched, roasted,
  and chopped

Soak dried fruit and raisins in cider overnight. Squeeze out, reserving extra cider, and dice fruit into bite-sized pieces. Add flour to reserved cider, and let stand overnight. Combine fruit and flour mixtures with all other ingredients, and beat well. The batter should be thick. Grease 12 to 14 small loaf pans (foil loaf pans about 6 × 3 ¼ × 2 inches are good). Fill pans to the top with dough. Cover with foil, and bake 1 ½ hours at 300°. Remove foil, and bake until the cake pulls away from sides of pans and is firm. Remove from oven and cool on racks. This fruitcake keeps well.

Laura and Guy Waterman of East Corinth, Vermont have hiked and climbed extensively in New England and also in the Bugaboos, Newfoundland, and Alaska. Most of their outings are in winter; during the summer they are busy on their farm. Guy has climbed all forty-six 4000-foot peaks in the White Mountains at least ten times each. He is the second person to have climbed both the White Mountains' "46" and the Adirondacks' "46" in winter. Laura was the first woman to make a winter ascent of New England's highest cliff, the Black Dike on Cannon Mountain, and to lead Pinnacle Gully in Huntington Ravine on Mt. Washington.

❝ On mountain outings we try to keep cost, weight, and volume low, provide good nutrition, and have meals that we really look forward to. The fruitcake recipe is rather complicated, but on winter hikes this cake is especially tasty, moist but not too rich.

For main dishes we prefer inexpensive grains, legumes, and vegetables to freeze-dried foods. We usually add a soup and a couple of hot drinks. Over the years when cooking and eating in tents, we have safely passed hundreds of cups of boiling hot liquids over sleeping bags and bodies. But luck finally ran out on a March trip to the Great Gulf Wilderness, a remote valley tucked among the highest peaks of New Hampshire's Presidential Range. A seemingly mad cup broke loose from our grasp and made a wild flight over our sleeping bags. Everyone in its path was severely burned. ❞

Fruit and Candy Confections

*"Look Fred, I don't care if your uncle **is** California's leading prune grower, you **don't** get to plan the menus again!"*

Gene Fear
TASTY TRAIL ENERGY BALLS

2 ¼ cups (1 pound) homogenized peanut butter
6 ½ cups (1 pound) dry milk
1 cup brown sugar
1 to 2 cups granola (to taste)

Mix thoroughly and form into balls. Wrap each ball individually.

Gene Fear of Tacoma, Washington is a backpacker and mountaineer whose specialty is conducting nationwide workshops that focus on survival. Besides giving lectures and writing articles on this subject, he is the author of two books, *Outdoor Living* and *Surviving the Unexpected Wilderness Emergency*, which deal with wilderness survival, natural disasters, man-made problems, and general information for safe recreation-type travel away from civilization. He has also been a consultant and an officer for various emergency, rescue, and safety organizations.

❝ What to eat isn't as much of a problem as the minimum equipment necessary for food preparation. An example is two climbers who had to give up an attempt on a major Peruvian peak because their only cooking pot blew away in a gust of wind. They were left with plenty of dehydrated food, but no way to prepare it, and with no container in which to melt snow for drinking water. Your blackened pot is your most valuable piece of equipment if you must evacuate hurriedly to escape a forest fire, flash flood, or other disaster. It is a tool for carrying water, for cooking, for digging latrines or snow caves, etc. Without the metal cook pot, the West would still be unexplored.

At present there seems to be a trend for rescue teams and desert travelers to use more and more peanut butter. I don't know why—probably convenience. Energy Balls are one of the latest peanut butter preparations. They're not bad, but I'm not sure what hot weather would do to them. ❞

Joan Firey
FRUIT-NUT ROLLS

Dried fruits and nuts in equal amounts (good combinations include raisins/walnuts, dates/pecans, and apricots/almonds)

Grind the fruit and nuts in a meat grinder. Mix well. Roll into balls 1 inch to 1½ inches in diameter. Wrap each ball in foil.

The late Joan Firey of Seattle, Washington was involved in alpine and expedition climbing from 1948 until shortly before her death in early 1980. She was also a skilled mountain artist and outdoor cook. Joan made numerous ascents, including many firsts, in the Cascades and in the Coast and Interior ranges of Canada. Her favorite mountaineering area was the Picket Range in the North Cascades, where she made the first winter ascent of Mt. Terror in 1977. Joan also climbed in California, Alaska, Mexico, and Peru. In 1978 she was a member of the American Women's Himalayan Expedition that put two women and two Sherpas on the summit of 26,545-foot Annapurna I.

Joan was in charge of the high altitude menus for the Annapurna expedition. She also wrote the section on alpine cuisine for the second and third editions of *Mountaineering: The Freedom of the Hills.*

❝I consider myself a mountain portrait painter. All my art work is outdoor related, whether of small details of flowers and trees, or rocks, or mountain panoramas. I am primarily a watercolorist, though I also work in acrylics and oils and do some serigraphs.

As to meals for backpacking and climbing, I feel that lunch munching is important, and so is choosing lunch foods to suit a variety of conditions (length of day, type of activity, weather, etc.). Sandwiches are fine. Fresh fruits and vegetables are a nice addition in summer. Richer, heavier foods are needed in winter. I always weigh my lunch foods, especially for trips longer than a weekend—important because lunch food can easily equal or surpass the weight of dehydrated breakfasts and dinners. Ten ounces of carefully planned lunch food per day is adequate to generous, though on long trips I allow more to accommodate increased appetites. Choose from meats, cheeses, nuts, dried fruits, breads, crackers, candies, and beverage mixes. My specialty for extended trips or bivouac climbs is the following mixture, which looks terrible but is a real sustainer. Mix thoroughly a 4½-ounce meat bar, 4½ ounces peanut butter, and 4 ounces of raisins ground in a meat grinder. Form into 3 or 4 portions and wrap in foil.❞

Ron and Lou Goudie
SNOWSHOE ENERGY BARS

1 cup powdered (confectioners' or
    icing) sugar
1 cup peanut butter
1 cup dates, finely chopped
1 cup nuts, chopped
4 to 5 tablespoons cream or evaporated
    milk

4 1-ounce squares semisweet chocolate
1 tablespoon butter
1 tablespoon melted paraffin
    (household wax for canning)

Mix sugar, peanut butter, dates, nuts, and cream in a bowl. With hands, shape mixture into small bars. In a double boiler, or in a saucepan over very low heat, melt chocolate, butter, and paraffin. Dip each bar into the chocolate mixture, and let dipped bars harden on cookie sheet. Wrap each bar in plastic wrap.

Ron and Lou Goudie, who live near Ottawa in Touraine, Quebec are among the quarter-million Canadians who enjoy snowshoeing. Ron has served for many years as assistant to the secretary of the Union Canadienne des Raquetteurs (Canadian Snowshoers' Union). He also represents snowshoers in the Sports Federation of Canada and is president of the International Snowshoe Union, which includes over a hundred clubs in Canada and the United States. Ron is particularly interested in competitive snowshoeing.

❝ During the winter, the snowshoe clubs hold contests. Men, women, and children compete in events similar to those in track and field. Participants wear moccasins and regulation racing snowshoes. International conventions, held annually on alternate sides of the border, are especially picturesque—each club has its particular colors and uniforms consisting of tuque, sash, tunic, and pants. Wearing or carrying their snowshoes, hundreds of snowshoers march in the parades. Competitive snowshoers are so serious that summers they keep in condition by jogging and sprinting with snowshoes on sandy beaches that simulate snow conditions.

Recreational snowshoeing also is a wonderful family activity. Just outside our town, in the Gatineau Hills, the Canadian Government has established seventy miles of trails for ski tourers and snowshoers, with warming and rest huts on major trails in Gatineau Park. In Quebec alone, 150,000 people come out on snowshoes each winter. It seems fitting that snowshoes are so popular in an area where they were vital to early-day winter travel.

We sometimes go out at night for variety. On one beautiful and unforgettable moonlit evening, we met a pair of timber wolves that had wandered down from the north country. They were as surprised as we were—none of us lingered. ❞

"Charlene, did you remember to put a pad under the stove?"

Elizabeth L. Horn
BASIC FRUIT LEATHER

Fresh fruit in any amount (Juicy varieties are best. Strawberries and rhubarb are
*   deliciously tingly and sour.)*
Sugar to taste

Place fruit, including skin and rinds, in blender and liquefy. Add sugar. Bring
mixture to a boil. Cool slightly. Spoon thinly and evenly on pieces of plastic wrap. Let
dry for several days—in the sun, in a dry warm climate; or on a table under the heat
of several gooseneck lamps, in a damp locality. The fruit leather is done when it can be
peeled up from the plastic sheet. Roll it up in the plastic, and store in refrigerator. It
keeps well for several months. For variety, sprinkle powdered sugar or shredded
coconut over the leather while it is still wet.

Elizabeth L. (Beth) Horn, a native of Indiana, lives with her husband, Kirk, in Boring, Oregon, east of Portland. She works in communications for the U.S. Forest Service in Portland. Beth is also a writer-photographer who specializes in books on alpine wild flowers. She is the author of *Wildflowers 1: The Cascades, Wildflowers 3: The Sierra Nevada*, and *Wildflowers: The Pacific Coast*.

❝ Fruit leather is easy to make for mountain and river trips, and so is dried fruit. It is also easy to make a food drier. All you need is an enclosed box (we use an old upright freezer), some wire shelves (hardware cloth or mesh fencing), a heat source (such as ordinary light bulbs), and ventilation (for instance, a small electric fan). We especially like dried apples and pears. To prepare fruit for drying, cut it into quarter-inch or thinner slices, and lay the slices on the wire shelves with the lights and fan turned on. It should dry in a few days, the exact time depending on the juice content of the fruit and other variables. ❞

Jon Van Zyle
FIVE-POUND FUDGE

1 13-ounce can evaporated milk
4 cups sugar
3 4-ounce bars sweet chocolate (baking variety) broken into small pieces
1 18-ounce package chocolate chips or morsels
1 7-ounce jar marshmallow creme
¼ cup (⅛ pound) butter or margarine)
1 to 2 cups chopped walnuts or pecans

Bring milk and sugar to boil in a very large saucepan. Stirring constantly, simmer at the boiling point for 7 minutes. Remove from heat, and quickly add sweet chocolate, chocolate chips, marshmallow creme, and butter. Stir until chocolate is dissolved and ingredients are well mixed. Add nuts. Pour into buttered pan or casserole, and cool. Refrigerate for 8 hours before cutting. For variety, sprinkle the nuts over the top of the fudge as it cools, instead of stirring them in.

Jon Van Zyle, an artist and outdoorsman, lives in Eagle River, Alaska about thirty miles from Anchorage. His acrylics of Alaskan scenes and situations hang in many galleries and private collections and have been reproduced in *Alaska* magazine, as well as in many others.

❝Through the years I have viewed and absorbed the splendor of pristine landscapes from one end of the state to the other—the real Alaska: now-vanished villages with their silent totem poles telling tales of a forgotten era and people, forest-bordered lakes, abandoned line shacks, the stark loneliness of the northern frontier.

I have always had dogs, and my wife, Charlotte, and I raise registered Siberian huskies. I have twice raced my dogs in the Iditarod dogsled races from Anchorage to Nome, a distance of 1150 to 1500 miles across the interior of Alaska. Strict rules govern the race—there are twenty-four checkpoints—and the trail is a testing ground for all kinds of things. The race usually takes two to four weeks. The racers are outdoors the whole time in temperatures that, with the windchill factor, can range from 40° to 80° below zero, or lower. When you are racing a sled, you run about 40 percent of the time. For both training and racing, you need snack food that is extremely high in energy and light in bulk. This snack, coupled with good nutritional protein and high-calorie food, sustains a good diet.❞

Barbara Roach
DRIED FRUIT ROLLS

1 pound dried dates
1 pound dried figs
1 pound raisins
1 pound dried apricots
1 pound shredded coconut
2 cups chopped pecans (or other nuts,
    to taste)

2 cups sugar
1½ cups cream
About ¼ cup (⅛ pound) butter (egg
    size)

Grind fruits and nuts and set aside in a bowl. Put sugar, cream, and butter in a saucepan and boil till mixture forms a soft ball when tested in ice water (the mixture should reach 234° to 240° on a candy thermometer). Add ground fruits and nuts. Stir well. Remove from heat, and spread onto a 24 × 24 inch cookie sheet. Cool, and cut into bars. Wrap bars in wax paper, and store in refrigerator for 1 month before taking on outing.

Barbara Roach of Durango, Colorado has been climbing mountains ever since she met her husband, Gerry, in 1966. The couple's many ascents include 19,550-foot Mt. Logan, the highest peak in Canada; 22,834-foot Aconcagua in Argentina; 17,400-foot Mt. Foraker in Alaska, by a new route, the North Ridge; and a first traverse of 16,523-foot Mt. Blackburn in Alaska. Both Barbara and Gerry were members of the American Bicentennial Everest Expedition that put two men on the summit of Everest in 1976.

❦❦ Like most husband-wife climbing teams, Gerry and I have developed a routine that works for us. Most of the time I plan, prepare, and cook all the food for our trips. On expeditions I don't mind doing 95 percent of the cooking if someone else will do 5 percent of it and also do most of the other camp chores.

Occasional mishaps do occur. One summer, at the end of five weeks' climbing in various parts of the United States, I was trying to use up the leftovers that had accumulated in numerous unlabeled plastic bags. I made up some vanilla-flavored breakfast mix for Gerry. It seemed a little thick, but I gave it to him. His comment was, 'It's terrible. Tastes like instant potatoes.' Sure enough, that's what it was! It pays to taste unidentified products before preparing.

If I could, I would have all fresh foods for expeditions. I haven't figured out how to do that, but I have sprouted alfalfa seeds on glaciers. Soak alfalfa seeds in brown vitamin jars, overnight or for a day. If left in a sun-warmed tent, they'll sprout an inch or more in ten hours. They taste really good! ❞

"That was either strawberry pudding or beef paprika."

George Willig
FRUIT PUFFS

1 cup dates, pitted	2 teaspoons sesame seeds (or 2 egg
½ cup raisins	whites mixed with ½ cup
¼ cup dried apricots	cornstarch)
¼ cup peanut butter	Oil for deep frying

Chop up dates, raisins, and apricots, and mix with peanut butter. Form into walnut-sized balls. Roll balls in sesame seeds or in egg white and cornstarch mixture. In oil preheated to 375°, fry balls till they are nicely browned.

George Willig of Los Angeles, California became interested in mountaineering and rock climbing in the early 1970's. His climbing career — interrupted for a year by a serious back problem — includes ascents in the North Cascades, the Sierra Nevada, Yosemite Valley, the Tetons, Canyonlands and Zion national parks in Utah, and in New Hampshire, Maine, New York, West Virginia, and Boulder, Colorado, where the Flatirons are located. In 1977 while a resident of Queens, a borough of New York on Long Island, George soloed the sheer "face" of the 1350-foot World Trade Center in New York City. This feat met with disapproval by New York authorities and also led to various television appearances for George. *Going It Alone*, by George Willig and Andrew Bergman, was published in 1979.

❝ I have hiked and backpacked since I was eleven years old. When I was fourteen I went on my first white-water canoe trip.Later I made several extended canoe trips in Algonquin Provincial Park in Ontario, Canada. In 1973, climbing became my major interest.

Usually when I am backpacking or climbing, I don't like to cook because it often entails carrying extra weight. In winter, though, cooking becomes necessary, or I may cook often on a leisurely canoe trip. Fruit Puffs go well on climbs, and I also like Peanut Butter Chew. Make it with 1 cup peanut butter, 1 cup honey, and 2 cups dry skim milk (use more milk if desired, but start out with 2 cups). Add some wheat germ if you so desire. Mix ingredients well with a wooden spoon, and wrap the wad in plastic. To eat, just tear some off and chew. It is high in protein and tastes good. ❞

Granolas and Gorps

"Mack, I think it's time you threw away your gorp!"

Tom Frost
HOMEMADE GRANOLA

2 ½ cups rolled cereals (to taste; use
   oatmeal alone, or combine it with
   rolled wheat and rolled rye from
   health food stores)
¼ cup sesame seeds
¼ cup sunflower seeds
½ cup coconut flakes or shreds
¼ cup wheat germ

½ cup sliced almonds
⅛ cup date sugar or ¼ cup brown
   sugar
½ cup water
⅓ cup honey
⅓ cup oil (soy or safflower)
Brewer's yeast, lecithin granules, and
   whey powder (optional)

*Mix dry ingredients. Stir in water, honey, and oil. Spread in shallow pan. Bake 2
hours at 225°. Cool. For a moister granola, use more honey and oil. Eat dry or mixed
with dry milk and water. If desired for additional nutrition, add brewer's yeast,
lecithin, and a little whey powder just before eating.*

Tom Frost, who with his wife, Dorene, lives in Boulder, Colorado is a
sailor-turned-mountaineer. He left championship boat racing behind after
he became interested in climbing at Stanford University. Tom worked for a
decade in Ventura, California with Yvon Chouinard, designing and manufacturing climbing equipment. He is now a free-lance cameraman for
documentary films. Tom is a recent vice-president of the American Alpine
Club. He and Dorene conduct family treks in Nepal.

❝ I have made various first or second ascents of Yosemite's Big Walls—
the Northwest Face of Half Dome, the Northwest Face of the Higher
Cathedral Spire, and several routes on Sentinel Rock and El Capitan. I have
put up new routes in the Chamonix/Mont Blanc area, in the Cordillera
Blanca of Peru, and on Lotus Flower Tower in the Northwest Territories. In
Nepal, in 1963 I made a first ascent of 22,340-foot Kantega with part of Sir
Edmund Hillary's schoolhouse expedition; in 1970 I reached 25,000 feet as a
member of the Annapurna South Face Expedition; and in 1979 I led a filming
expedition to the summit of 22,494-foot Ama Dablam in the Everest area.
    Food needs vary. On Yosemite's granite walls we used to specialize in
salami, cheese, hard rolls, chocolate, gorp, and water. Water and most
foods were rationed, but never gorp (no need—it is very unpalatable on a
thirsty wall). At high altitudes with very little oxygen, much stress, and
great energy output, you need digestible nutritious food and wide variety.
Dorene's granola (with my addition of brewer's yeast, lecithin, and maybe a
little whey powder) has kept me moving over many a trail and pass. And
Dorene never lets a special occasion go unobserved. On my birthday in
1969, at 14,000 feet on McKinley, she produced from her personal pack
canned pound cake, dried strawberries, and whipped cream—my favorite
dessert! ❞

Chet Marler
ENCHANTMENT GRANOLA

6 cups quick oatmeal
¾ cup wheat germ
½ cup coconut (flaked or shredded)
½ cup brown sugar
⅓ cup sesame or sunflower seeds

1 cup nuts (chopped walnuts or pecans,
or peanuts)
½ cup salad oil
⅓ cup honey
1 ½ teaspoons vanilla

In oven heat oatmeal in a shallow pan at 350° for about 10 minutes. Combine toasted oatmeal, wheat germ, coconut, sugar, seeds, and nuts. Add oil, honey, and vanilla. Spread on shallow pan. Heat in oven at 350° for 20 to 25 minutes; stir every 5 minutes to brown evenly. Cool, then stir until crumbly. Makes about 10 cups. Excellent for breakfasts, with or without milk. (Chopped dry fruit can be added to mix after roasting and cooling.)

Chet Marler of Leavenworth, Washington is a mountaineer, ski tourer, and alpine skier. He is employed by the Leavenworth Ranger District of the U.S. Forest Service.

❞ One of my outdoor objectives is to make ski runs from the summits of all the volcanic cones in Washington State. I have skied down Mt. Adams and also down Glacier Peak via the Sitkum Glacier.

On backpacks, quickie recipes are very useful. For one quick dinner, I cook instant rice, open a can of sardines, drain off the oil, and add the sardines to the rice. Grated cheese over the top adds a nice garnish. If sardines don't suit your taste buds, substitute shrimp, salmon, or tuna. For another easy meal, I combine instant rice, instant bean soup mix, and an appropriate amount of water. As it heats, I stir in small pieces of diced ham (canned or freeze-dried) and sometimes add spices. ❞

Patricia Armstrong
GLORIOUS GORP

Cereals and grains —2 cups total from some of the following: wheat germ, oatmeal,
   prepared bran-morsel breakfast cereal, granola, birchermeusli, etc.
Fruits —2 ½ cups total from 3 or 4 of the following: raw cranberries;
   dried figs, pears, apples, peaches, apricots, bananas, dates, raisins, etc.
Seeds and chopped nuts —3 cups total from 3 or 4 of the following: sunflower seeds,
   sesame seeds, coconut, cashews, almonds, Brazil nuts, walnuts, filberts,
   macadamia nuts, peanuts, pecans, hickory nuts, etc.
42 ounces total (1 18-ounce and 2 12-ounce packages) of semisweet chocolate chips or
   morsels, butterscotch chips, and peanut butter flavored chips
1 tablespoon honey or molasses

Assemble dry ingredients. Chop up larger pieces of fruits and nuts. Mix dry ingredients together in large bowl. Melt chips or morsels in top of double boiler, stir in honey or molasses, and pour over cereals, fruits, and nuts. Mix well, and press or pour into buttered cookie sheets. Cool, and cut into 2 × 4 inch chunks. Wrap in plastic or foil. One pound of this high-energy mix will supply enough calories for a day's strenuous activity —plus all the protein, vitamins, minerals, and natural fiber needed

   Patricia (Pat) Stoddard Armstrong and her husband, Charles, live in Naperville, Illinois west of Chicago. Pat is a botanist, ecologist, teacher, and writer. In Alaska in the late 1960's, she participated in the Juneau Icefield Research Project and the Foundation for Glaciological Research Project — first as a graduate student and later as the first woman instructor.

   ❝I have climbed in most of the large mountain areas of the United States, Canada, Ecuador, Peru, and New Zealand, and soloed the four highest peaks in Mexico. Chuck and I lead outings each year for outdoor clubs. I never travel without my lightweight, compact backpacking herb/ spice kit, carried in empty film cans. I take four sets of flavorings, which do wonders for tired old leftovers and other backpack meals:
   1. a blend of sugar, cinnamon, clove, nutmeg, and ginger to use on bread, puddings, fruits, and cereals;
   2. a combination of garlic, paprika, oregano, basil, chili, and cumin — delicious on beef/Italian and Mexican foods;
   3. a mix of garlic, marjoram, thyme, rosemary, sage, caraway, and parsley for pork and poultry; and
   4. a mixture of onion, garlic, celery salt, parsley, oregano, and thyme that is good with eggs, cheese, milk, and vegetables.❞

"Gee, Elaine, maybe next time we should use just a **little** less garlic in the stew."

Ome Daiber
INSTANT MOUNTAIN ENERGY FOOD

1 cup instant whole wheat cereal
1 cup quick oatmeal
2 to 3 cups chopped dates
1 2 ½-ounce jar dried (chipped) beef

Preheat oven to 400°. Mix cereals and fruit and set aside. Remove meat from jar, separate slices, and spread on cookie sheet. Turn off oven and put in meat. Meat will dry out in about 15 minutes—take care it doesn't scorch. Remove dried meat from oven. With rolling pin, crumble it into fine pieces. When it is cool, mix with other ingredients. Store and carry mixture in a covered plastic container. Eat dry by the handful for trail food, or mix with hot water for a tasty morning or evening meal.

Ome Daiber lives in Bothell, Washington near Seattle. He climbed extensively in the Cascades and Olympics as a Boy Scout and later. In the early 1930's he began developing and manufacturing outdoor equipment and supplies for climbers, arctic explorers, skiers, hunters, fishermen, scouts, and others. He was the first distributor of dehydrated foods in the Pacific Northwest and the nation. In 1936 he started a long career in mountain rescue work—as a volunteer on many rescues, and as a leader in organization and techniques. Ome is now in great demand as a speaker at survival seminars and as a teacher of outdoor skills.

One of Ome's many mountain ascents was his September 29-30, 1935 climb (with Arnie Campbell and Jim Borrow) of Mt. Rainier via Liberty Ridge, a steep demanding new route that was not repeated for twenty years. The summit view was unforgettable.

❝ We stood on the top of Liberty Cap...spellbound....The great shadow of the mountain cast by the setting sun was so solid a looking thing. It seemed as if we could walk out as far as the eye could reach....

The great peaks of the Northwest rose in gold...clear up into Canada and down into Oregon....

We could see the Puget Sound country with the water reflection picking up the light of the setting sun...islands and a couple of boats. And along the eastern horizon there was a thin black line....After a bit we realized that the thin black line was getting higher...coming closer and only then did we realize that it was night....

And finally, night came like the leaf of a book, and it was dark.

One thing I learned about food on Liberty Ridge—never carry cans of gasoline in the same pack with grub. Our sandwiches were date bread flavored with gasoline. ❞

Glenn Exum
SOELDRICK

1 cup raw oatmeal
1 cup brown sugar
1 cup peanuts
1 cup raisins
Hot cocoa mix, small amount (to taste)

Mix ingredients well. May be made in any amount to suit any size of party.

Glenn Exum of Moose, Wyoming lives in the afternoon shadow of the Teton Range. He is a pioneer climber who has had an influence on the lives of innumerable other climbers. In 1931, when he was a seventeen year old outfitted with leather-cleated football shoes, he soloed the Grand Teton by a new route that later was named the Exum. Since then he has climbed the Grand some 300 times, in addition to making many other ascents in Wyoming, Canada, and the Alps. In 1935 he was the first American to solo the Matterhorn.

Glenn climbed for years with Paul Petzoldt, in whose guide service and mountaineering school he was a guide and later a partner. When Petzoldt retired in the mid-1950's, Glenn took over the operation of the service. In 1971 and 1976, he invited some of his old friends to celebrate the 40th and 45th anniversaries of the first ascent of the Exum Ridge by repeating the route. He has since retired from the guide service, which has long been known as one of the oldest continuously run such services in the country.

The late Willi Unsoeld, a former Teton guide, when asked what he thought Glenn was most noted for, replied, "His ability to hold a guide concession together all these years with all the changes that have come in the climbing world. He had to deal with many strong-willed personalities (I was one of them), but he just kept on going. One thing that accounts for his success is that Glenn is such a gentleman. He never had a bad word to say about anyone."

❝ The recipe for Soeldrick was devised by Willi Unsoeld and his wife, Jolene, when they were going together—the name is a combination of his last name and her maiden name, Bishoprick. Another recipe that climbers always like is Alpine Ice Cream. Mix jam and snow together, and stir vigorously. ❞

Dee Molenaar
PAPAYA-LICORICE GORP

Peanuts	*Dried pears*
Raisins	*Licorice-flavored candies or gumdrops*
Dried papaya	*Small chocolate candies with*
Dried pineapple	*variegated color coating*

Mix ingredients in any amounts needed and in any proportions, to taste. Dried papaya and pineapple can be found in the gourmet sections of health food stores; they give a little different flavor to trail food.

Dee Molenaar of Burley, Washington is a veteran climber of varied and extensive experience. In 1946 he was with an expedition that was the second to climb 18,008-foot Mt. St. Elias on the Alaska-Canada boundary (at least nine previous attempts had been made on St. Elias, the only successful one led by the Duke of Abruzzi fifty years before). In 1953, Dee was on the American expedition that reached 25,000 feet on the world's second highest peak, 28,250-foot K2 in the Karakoram Range in Pakistan. In March 1965 he was with a party that accompanied Senator Robert F. Kennedy on the first ascent of Mt. Kennedy in the Yukon Territory, a 13,905-foot peak which the Canadian government had recently named after the late President John F. Kennedy. The ascent was made in connection with the National Geographic Society/Boston's Museum of Science expedition that was mapping that section of the St. Elias Mountains under the leadership of Bradford Washburn and Maynard Miller. In late 1980, Dee was in the Antarctic and New Zealand in connection with his pictorial map-making project.

Dee's name has long been associated with 14,410-foot Mt. Rainier. He served as a Rainier guide in the early 1940's and as a national park ranger during 1948-1952. He has climbed Rainier more than fifty times by at least twelve different routes, including several new routes. In 1957 the *American Alpine Journal* ran Dee's article, "Climbing History of Mount Rainier," which amounted to an early climbing guide. It was forerunner to his comprehensive volume, *The Challenge of Rainier*, first published in 1971 and revised and expanded in 1980; included are many pencil sketches by the author, who is also a mountain artist of note.

❝ A somewhat startling food incident, 'The Case of the Instant Flambeau Dinner,' occurred when Forrest Johnson and I were climbing Mt. Adams. I made the mistake of carrying drinking water and gasoline in identical plastic bottles. You can imagine what followed. When preparing dinner, I realized what had happened when a flame flickered over the surface of the soup in a pot. ❞

Finis Mitchell
BULK-AND-CHEW WILDERNESS FOOD

*¼ cup natural wheat-barley prepared
  breakfast cereal*
¼ cup oatmeal for babies
¼ cup rice cereal for babies
*¼ cup high-protein prepared breakfast
  cereal*
¼ cup dry milk

2 tablespoons wheat germ
3 tablespoons nondairy creamer
2 teaspoons sugar
*¼ cup finely chopped dry fruit (dates,
  raisins, prunes), or nuts
  (preferably cashews, or others to
  taste)*

*Mix all ingredients together. This mix has bulk and chew and is a satisfying breakfast
or emergency food.*

Finis Mitchell lives in Rock Springs, Wyoming. Since 1909, he has hiked 13,000 miles and climbed some 250 peaks in the Wind River Range of Wyoming. In the 1930's, he and his father ran a fishing resort on the west side of the range, and planted two-and-a-half million fish—hauled on horseback—in 314 lakes. To honor this service, 12,482-foot Mt. Mitchell bears the family name. Finis has written a guidebook, *Wind River Trails*, and his articles and photographs have appeared in outdoor magazines. He takes thousands of color slides each summer. Winters, he gives illustrated lectures, with an emphasis on this country's wilderness heritage. In 1977 the University of Wyoming awarded Finis an honorary doctorate for his "outstanding service in the field of environmental awareness and conservation."

❝ In 1952 apparently no one had ever attempted to explore Fremont Gorge. In July that year I set out alone from what is now Elkhart Park, with seventy-eight pounds in my old surplus army pack. Bypassing a lake dammed up by an old rock slide, I tried to climb down a big spruce to get over a sixty-foot ledge. The lower limbs broke, and I fell to the ground. My life was saved because I landed on top of my pack. I spent four-and-a-half hours crawling under massive boulders, dragging my pack behind. I named that lake Suicide Lake; its name is on maps to this day.

I ran out of food two days before my scheduled pickup. I had to climb up a glacier neck between what are now called Turret and Sunbeam peaks, and down a vicious rock chute onto Dinwoody Glacier. I caught some nice brook trout—but above 10,600 feet in the Wind Rivers, there is no wood, not even a shrub. I cut up the fish and cooked them in my little pan with only dead grass and flower leaves for fuel. A leaf/grass fire also helped me once when the wind blew away my snow glasses. I smoked my eyeglasses. Then I couldn't see through them, so I erased a tiny spot in the center. It worked. ❞

Jerky, Pemmican, and Toast

Frank Ashley
BEEF JERKY

1½ pounds lean beef (flank or round steak)	1 teaspoon seasoned salt
	½ teaspoon onion powder
½ cup Worcestershire sauce	½ teaspoon garlic powder
½ cup soy sauce	¼ teaspoon pepper

Remove all fat from the meat (otherwise it will spoil). Cut meat into quarter-inch slices along the grain (easier if meat is partially frozen). Combine liquid and dry ingredients to make marinade. Marinate meat overnight in refrigerator, in stainless steel pan or shallow glass dish. Next day drain off marinade. Lay strips of meat in single layer on oven rack (no overlap), with foil on rack below to catch drippings. Set oven at 150°, and leave door ajar. In a gas oven warmed by a pilot light, dry meat at 150° for about 6 hours; then turn off heat, and leave meat in the oven for 6 more days. With an electric oven, roast meat for 8 to 12 hours, or until it is as dry and chewy as desired. Remove meat from oven, and store in tightly closed glass jars in refrigerator or other cool place. This amount makes about ½ pound jerky. The recipe can be doubled or tripled if there is room in the oven.

Frank Ashley, who lives near Culver City, California operates an alpine guide service and leads backpack outings throughout the West. He also conducts backpacking seminars in Southern California, lectures, and publishes a monthly newsletter for backpackers. A free-lance writer, he has contributed to various outdoor publications. His book, *Highpoints of the States*, is based on his 1969 record of reaching the highest summit in each of the "connected forty-eight states" during a period of 112 days.

❝ The late Vin Hoeman of Alaska is recognized as the first person to scale (over several years) the high points of all fifty states. I am an avid map reader, and one day while looking at some maps I got to thinking about that idea. I thought for five years. Then, with some sponsorship and with the cooperation of my wife and family, I did all the highest elevations in one season.

I have climbed and backpacked for over twenty years—in the Sierra Nevada especially, elsewhere in the United States (including Alaska), and in Canada, Mexico, and Ecuador. One of my important cooking tools on backpacks is a long-handled wooden spoon—it's light in weight and prevents burned fingers. The mountain meal that sticks in my memory as most memorable was in Ecuador one Thanksgiving Day, on the lower slopes of 20,563-foot Chimborazo. I was sitting outside an Indian hut, with a native sheepherder and his flock nearby. My meal was a can of Ecuadorian stew—cold because I couldn't get my stove going! ❞

June Fleming
SPICED PEMMICAN

½ cup raisins
½ cup dates
½ cup dried apricots
½ cup dried beef (in jar or plastic
    envelope)
Peel of 1 orange
¾ cup brown sugar
½ to 1 teaspoon each cinnamon,
    nutmeg, and allspice

Pinch salt
1 teaspoon vanilla
1 tablespoon each vinegar, oil, and
    maple syrup
½ of a beaten egg
½ cup flour
Sufficient amount of cider, brandy, or
    rum to make a heavy dough

Chop fine the dried fruits, dried beef, and orange peel. Mix these ingredients thoroughly with the sugar, spices, flavorings, vinegar, oil, syrup, egg, and flour. Work in enough cider, brandy, or rum to make a heavy dough. Put dough into an 8-inch square pan. Bake at 325° for an hour or longer, until it sets well and isn't too sticky. Cut into squares and wrap. Spiced Pemmican keeps well for several weeks. This is a modern version of the old buffalo meat and serviceberry staple. It is very rich, compact, and high in calories—a little goes a long way. It is good for breakfasts, snacks, and emergencies.

June Fleming of Portland, Oregon teaches outdoor subjects for Portland Community College, the Park Bureau, and the YWCA (Young Women's Christian Association). She wrote *The Well-Fed Backpacker* and *Games (and More!) for Backpackers*, edited *The Outdoor Idea Book*, and has presented local television programs on winter camping.

❝ Topics covered in my outdoor classes include backpacking, snow camping, edible wild plants, and food drying. For fun, besides backpacking, I do nature photography and go cross-country skiing and snow camping. In 1975 three friends and I skied almost the entire length of the Oregon Cascades, from Timberline Lodge on Mt. Hood south to Lake of the Woods near Klamath Falls. During our ski trip, record heavy snows fell—it snowed for thirty-seven out of the forty-two days we were out. However, we had planned for months, and our thoroughness was rewarded by a satisfying trip with no major mishaps.

While we were traveling and living in snow for six weeks, a lot of our civilized layer of couth dropped away. Near Waldo Lake we stood around eating a delicious dinner of brown rice, peppers, cheese sauce, bacon bar, and dried tomatoes. The temperature was so cold that our noses dripped constantly—we finally just gave up trying to wipe them. We wondered whether the same meal would taste nearly as good back home, ungarnished by drips. ❞

Morris Jenkins
FRUIT-NUT PEMMICAN

2 cups mixed nuts
1½ cups raisins
8 ounces dried dates

8 ounces dried beef or jerky
Honey to make stiff dough
Salt to taste

Grind up nuts, raisins, dates, and meat. Mix thoroughly in large bowl. Stir in enough honey to give the mixture the consistency of stiff dough. Add salt if needed (some kinds of dried beef or jerky contain enough salt). Pack in double plastic bags, and store in a durable paper bag or a covered ice cream container for protection in pack. A tablespoon of this pemmican between 2 slices of bread makes a satisfying meal.

Morris Jenkins of Cle Elum, Washington was a professional forester for over forty years and a backpacker longer than that.

❝ My wife, Sue, and I spent our honeymoon in 1932 in the Cascades north of Cle Elum. One day we started uptrail with no packs and only a sandwich between us. We got to a rugged rock spire between Hyas and Deep lakes, now called Cathedral Rock. Then it was known as Jimmy's Jumpoff—after Jimmy Grieve, an early-day gold miner, who had once backpacked a woodstove from Fish Lake to his cabin behind the spire.

Nobody in our area had any climbing equipment in the early 1930's. We just decided to climb the 6724-foot spire. It was difficult going in places. About 150 feet from the top, there was a chockstone in a chimney. I got past the obstacle, Sue came up, and in a short time we scrambled to the top. There was a register then, and as far as we know Sue was the first woman to make the climb.

By then it was quite late. Down near Peggy's Pond we could see Jimmy's old cabin. We reached the cabin just before dark, with hopes of finding food. There was some flour in a can, but it was so ancient it had turned yellow; the pancakes I made were inedible. Grouse season was open, but I had no gun. I managed to hit a fool hen with a rock, and then cut it up to broil on sticks over the campfire. Sue claims it was cooked three ways—burned, raw, and well done; she couldn't force it down.

After spending the night curled up on an old mattress in the cabin, I managed to eat a little more grouse—but not so Sue. We then climbed 7986-foot, glacier-covered Mt. Daniel. We came down the cliffs above Hyas Lake, only to find there was no shoreline. Luckily I spotted a raft nearby, so I poled us across to the Fish Lake trail. That night we spent in a ranger's cabin where I had left ample food when on a Forest Service job. But Sue was too tired to eat. It was quite an experience to do all that on one sandwich and a couples of bites of fool hen. ❞

Lee Nading
DRIED FRUIT PEMMICAN BARS

Dried fruits, any amount of every kind desired
Nuts, kinds and quantities to taste
Powdered sugar

Put the dried fruits and nuts through a coarse meat grinder. Spread the mixture out on a cookie sheet and cut into bars. Cover loosely and let stand for about 2 weeks, until rather dried out. Dust with powdered sugar. Wrap bars individually in foil, and refrigerate. These bars are somewhat neutral in flavor (like stale raisins), but are easy to make, nutritious, and compact.

Lee Nading of Bloomington, Indiana has backpacked for a decade in midwestern wilderness areas and western desert backcountry. Out of his experiences he authored plastic Survival Cards crammed with facts of use to outdoorsmen all over the world.

❝ I discovered that a truly compact, indestructible survival manual did not exist. I started collecting basic survival facts on 3 × 5 cards to carry in my pack. From this beginning, the small-print plastic format seemed to follow logically. The published cards are probably the most condensed, comprehensive survival guide available. They give basic information on shelter, water, fire, wild edibles, first aid, equipment, hunting, trapping, fishing, emergency signals, orientation, etc. They cover data for all climatic zones — arctic, temperate, tropic, and desert. The cards fit handily into luggage, pack, survival kit, or shirt pocket.

I am also interested in conservation and actively promoted the establishment of the Indiana Wilderness Area in the 722,000-acre Hoosier National Forest of south-central Indiana. I also originated the concept for the proposed Tecumseh Trail, a 3500-mile hiking route from Manitoba to Florida. I have made a large hand-drawn map of the Hoosier National Forest and several maps for outdoor books.

My backpack menus vary a good deal, depending on the type of trip and environmental conditions. In summer, especially in desert areas, I take along foods with zesty flavors, such as orange flavor instant drink, very spicy jerky, and sweets of all kinds. Fruit Pemmican Bars suit all kinds of trips and conditions. ❞

Glen Boles
BACON-TOAST SANDWICHES

4 slices bread
Butter, liberal amount
6 to 8 slices bacon

Fry bacon, and drain off grease. Meanwhile toast bread, and spread the hot toast liberally with butter. Make sandwiches as soon as the bacon is done, let cool, and package for trip. These keep well for days. Toast sandwiches might sound dry, but they are just right.

Glen W. Boles was born and brought up in New Brunswick, where he acquired a love of the outdoors and athletics from his father. He moved west to Calgary, Alberta in 1953. In the late 1950's, mountain guide Heinz Kahl introduced him to climbing—a blend of athletics and the out-of-doors. Glen has made numerous climbs in the Selkirks, Purcells, and Bugaboos, and in the Rocky Mountains of Canada (including ascents of the range's four highest summits, all between 12,000 and 13,000 feet elevation—Clemenceau, North Twin, Columbia, and Robson).

In 1967, Glen was a member of the Yukon Alpine Centennial Expedition, a Canadian-American party organized to commemorate the 100th anniversary of the Confederation of Canada and the United States' purchase of Alaska. The group made the first ascent of a 15,700-foot peak on the Yukon/Alaska border, dubbed "Good Neighbor Peak," an unclimbed summit of Mt. Vancouver in the St. Elias Range. Glen has also climbed in the Alps, is active in the Calgary Mountain Rescue Group, is a mountain photographer and artist, and is a coauthor of *A Climber's Guide to the Rocky Mountains of Canada—South*.

❝ On backpacking trips my pals and I carry a jackknife, spoon, bowl, and cup apiece, plus the community gear of stirring spoon, scouring pad, and necessary pots (all meals are boiled, for easier cleanup). Group breakfasts and dinners are made up ahead of time. Each member of the party is responsible for preparing and carrying specific meals. In this way we get a good variety.

In a small nylon bag I take lots of goodies to nibble on—raisins, nuts, candies, chocolate, jerky, and dried fruits. They keep up energy when I am on the move and also serve as emergency rations in case of a longer stay than expected. A few years ago I got the idea from Don Forest, one of my climbing partners, of making the basic part of all lunches beforehand and packaging each day's individually. Toast is my mainstay. I like it best with bacon; but sometimes I just butter the toast and take cheese, sausage, or sardines to eat with it. ❞

Camp-Cooked Meals

PART TWO

Camp~Cooked Meals

One-pot concoctions are the most popular, versatile, and practical of all camp meals, both in preparation and eating. A lightweight pot, in about a one-and-a-half quart size, with a cover, is adequate for two or three people, although a second pot comes in handy. Fried or baked foods are delicious, but more time and trouble are involved; gear for these cooking methods should include a frying pan, preferably with a well fitting cover, and spatula. Foods with perishable ingredients have a place on many trips, but must be kept cold and eaten early to avoid the possibility of food poisoning.

Most dishes in this section can be cooked on a one-burner stove. A few are better done over a campfire, which nowadays, at least in the United States, is not always permitted or possible.

Elevation influences food preparation in various ways. The most noticeable effect is the extra time required to prepare boiled foods. At sea level, water boils at 212° F; at 5000 feet elevation, at 203° F; at 10,000 feet, at 194° F. In practical terms, the cooking time for many boiled foods doubles with every 5000 feet of elevation gain—and some products will never get done at high altitudes.

The cooking time for baked foods does not vary much with altitude, but as the barometric pressure drops with increasing elevations, leavening agents such as baking powder, become more active. In camp baking, no correction is needed for this activity. Just enjoy the extra fluffiness of your baked foods. It is a beneficial offset to unpredictable conditions such as fluctuating temperatures.

Cups used in camp are nearly always larger than standard 8-ounce measuring cups, and camp spoons are usually outsize.

1 quart = 32 fluid ounces (4 standard measuring cups)

One-Pot Glops, Hooshes, Stews, and Soups

Donald N. Anderson
STRIKE-AGAIN MUNG

*Freeze-dried chicken or pork (any
   amount, to taste)*
1 quart water (more or less)
1 package chicken-noodle soup mix

1 package onion soup mix
2 to 3 cups minute (or instant) rice
1 package gravy mix (optional)
Flavorings, to taste

*Reconstitute meat according to directions on package. Bring water to boil, and add
reconstituted meat, soup mixes, rice, gravy mix, and flavorings. Stir occasionally.
Cook 20 minutes or until done. Time of cooking varies with elevation. Serves 2.*

Dr. Donald N. Anderson of Anchorage, Alaska has climbed and explored
for many years in the mountains of Washington and Alaska. His climbs have
included new routes and winter ascents in the Cascades and Olympics.

❝ This recipe is the only one I can remember that is worth repeating. I
started using it in the mid-1950's on trips with the Forever And Ever Boys, a
little-known group native to the Olympic Peninsula where I grew up. 'Strike
Again' is the FAEB motto.

Numerous variations are possible. I like it thin; but depending on the
quantity of water used, it will come out anywhere between a soup and a
very thick stew. Small tins of meat can be used instead of freeze-dried. Beef
Mung results from substituting canned or freeze-dried beef for the chicken
or pork, and beef-flavor soup mix for the onion and chicken-noodle. For
trips to the high mountains, on winter trips, or in very cold climates, heavy
slabs of margarine layered into the Mung increase the caloric content.

Mung has been served on many an outing in the Olympics and was eaten
on Mt. McKinley in 1960. The favorite Mung for many Forever And Ever
Boys is the version brewed up in 1966 to celebrate a new route on 14,573-foot
Mt. Hunter in the Alaska Range, when Donald W. Anderson and I made the
fourth ascent of Hunter via the Northeast Ridge. For our celebratory Mung,
we used traditional onion and chicken-noodle soup mixes, but instead of
meat we added a large tin of minced clams. Shavings from a big block of
cheddar cheese were melted in, and more cheese shavings were placed on
top as a garnish.

Even after five or six weeks in the mountains, it is not unusual for a
Forever And Ever boy to turn up his nose at a noodle or potato dish in favor
of a more traditional basic Mung. ❞

Bruce Beck
MISOSHIRU

Vegetables, fresh, freeze-dried, or
dehydrated: onion, garlic,
potatoes, cabbage, mushrooms,
spinach, etc., according to your
desire

1 pint water
½ teaspoon hondashi or kobucha
powder (optional)
1 tablespoon miso (or more to taste)

(Hondashi is Japanese instant soup stock. Kobucha is from dried seaweed. Miso is a soybean paste. Look for these in Japanese markets, or some supermarkets or health food stores.) Prepare fresh vegetables, and slice or cube; or reconstitute the dried vegetables. Put water on to heat, and add hondashi or kobucha powder. (If you have neither, fry vegetables in a little butter or oil before adding water.) Add vegetables and boil them till soft. On low heat, stir in miso. Heat just until a rolling boil has started. Take off heat. Don't boil after adding miso, or its delicate flavor is lost. Serves 2. This soup is simple to make, nutritious, and easy to pack.

Bruce Beck, formerly of New England and Canada, makes neoprene crampon straps and snowshoe bindings in his specialized outdoor business in Santa Barbara, California.

❝ I started this enterprise in New Hampshire, after living and climbing between the Selkirks and Purcells of British Columbia from 1963 to 1965. I had lived on a Vermont apple orchard from age six to eighteen and did a lot of tree climbing. I started rock and mountain climbing when I went to college in Rhode Island and continued it while I was at the University of Vermont. During that period Curt Beebe and I did a lot together in the Green Mountains of Vermont and in the Adirondacks in northeastern New York State. We went out in all kinds of weather and enjoyed hard going, with no trails; we made many winter and night ascents. Eventually we climbed all the forty-odd Adirondacks peaks over 4000 feet elevation. We also taught a little rock climbing and tried to encourage people to take overnight snowshoe trips and to bivouac with a minimum of equipment.

One of the most expeditious but revolting meals I remember was breakfast one morning when Curt and I planned to make a fast getaway on a seven-day snow traverse of the Cold River region in the Adirondacks. We made up our 'breakfast' the night before and stowed it in our packs while we slept on the luxurious straw of a lean-to. Early next morning we tried to eat four whole, cold, peanut butter sandwiches apiece. Although on the point of gagging, we got the stuff down with the help of water. But we did make an early start and had an ambitious trip, climbing many peaks along the way. **❞**

Lynn Buchanan
RAINIER SPOTTED DOG

3 cups water
Instant mashed potatoes
Cheddar cheese, shaved

2½ to 5 ounces dried (chipped) beef
Butter, salt, and pepper

Heat water. Add potatoes according to directions on package, in any amount necessary for preferred thickness. Add desired quantities of cheese, chipped beef, butter, and flavorings. Serves 2.

Lynn Buchanan of Yakima, Washington has made many climbs in the Cascades, including over twenty ascents of Mt. Adams by various routes, one in winter. He was in the group led by the late Hal Foss that first completed a high-level encirclement of Mt. Rainier at about the 9000-10,000-foot level. Lynn has taken part in countless mountain rescues, has been chairman of the Washington State Mountain Rescue Council and president of the Mountain Rescue Association, and was a recent director of the American Alpine Club.

Lynn was climb leader for ten of the eleven mass ascents of Mt. Adams held in the late 1960's and early 1970's. From Yakima, glacier-covered Adams, 12,276 feet high, is visible although it lies fifty airline miles to the southwest.

❝ The one-day climb, in late July, took six months' planning ahead each year. Between 400 and 500 people would sign up for the ascent. Most were from Yakima, but some came from all over the state and elsewhere. Local meetings and physical conditioning programs were held to prepare participants. Experienced climbers volunteered as leaders and arrived on the mountain days ahead to get everything ready. They marked the route (on the easy south side) with bamboo wands, set up radio communication and a first-aid station, and arranged for Mountain Rescue personnel to be on hand. I most enjoyed taking people up who really wanted to climb but had never had an opportunity. It was a relatively safe way to have a mountain adventure. Two hundred to 300 would reach the summit after a 6000-foot gain in elevation. Participants either got so tired they never wanted to climb again, or else became climbers from then on.

We had some humorous incidents. One fellow carried up a two-foot mirror to signal to his friends in Yakima. My younger brother had often heard our route referred to as so easy it was a 'grandmother's hike,' so he backpacked a rocking chair to the summit. He was among the first to arrive and rocked away in his chair as others finished the climb. We discouraged dogs after the time I returned to camp to find a dog wolfing down the steak I had been looking forward to all day. ❞

Esther Courtney
CHELAN CORNED BEEF HASH

Corned beef, 1 12-ounce can
Onion, chopped (preferably fresh —or dry) to taste
Seasonings to taste
Hashed brown potatoes (freeze-dried, or about half a 6-ounce package precooked
   dehydrated)

Heat meat, onion, and seasonings. Rehydrate potatoes in hot water, according to
package directions; drain if necessary. Add potatoes to meat. Stir and cook till
thoroughly mixed and well done. Serves 2.

Esther Courtney and her husband, Ray, live in a two-story log house on
the Stehekin River, just outside the North Cascades National Park boundary
and nine miles north of Stehekin Landing. The isolated town of Stehekin,
Washington, located in a national recreation area, is at the head of fifty-
mile-long Lake Chelan and can be reached only by boat, small plane, or
mountain trail.

Esther has walked thousands of miles over trails that lead in and out of
Stehekin. Since the late 1960's she has also been guide and cook for hiking
trips in the North Cascades.

❦❦ In winter Ray and I both lead cross-country ski trips. Summers, Ray
conducts pack trips by horseback into surrounding mountain areas, and I
lead trips for people who like to hike without carrying heavy packs. Tents,
supplies, and food go along by horse. Our sons and daughter all assist in the
family business.

For our trips I bake the bread we use, in my wood-burning range. I also
plant a large garden—with a high fence to keep the deer out—and grow
most of the vegetables used. Other food and supplies must be ordered well
ahead, since it is a fifty-mile, two-day round trip by boat to the nearest
supermarket. My hikers also come by boat. I often rendezvous with them at
jumping-off points into the wilderness. They usually arrive hungry!

On the trail, lunch frequently consists of peanut butter and jelly
sandwiches, summer sausage, cheese, gorp, a fresh orange, and either
water or a grapefruit or orange flavor instant drink. Another dinner that is
simple and delicious is made from macaroni, prepared according to package
directions, with a large amount of shredded cheddar cheese stirred in; the
cheese melts and forms a nice thick sauce. I do the cooking; but once a trip
begins, I never have to wash a dish—my guests won't let me. 99

Stella Degenhardt
TOMYHOI TUNA-NOODLES

3 cups water
½ teaspoon salt
1 package dried mixed vegetable flakes
    or freeze-dried vegetables

½ package instant cream of mushroom
    soup mix
1 cup noodles
1 6½-ounce can tuna

Put water, salt, vegetables, soup mix, and noodles into pot. Boil for 7 to 10 minutes, or until vegetables and noodles are done (cooking time varies with the altitude, etc.). Stir in tuna. (Dried vegetable flakes can be found in supermarket spice sections as "soup greens," and sometimes at mountaineering shops. Freeze-dried vegetables are carried by most mountaineering and backpacking stores.) Serves 2.

Stella Degenhardt of Seattle, Washington started hiking, ski mountaineering, and climbing in the early 1950's. Her climbs include a new route on Yellow Jacket Tower in the Cascades, via the south face, and a first ascent of 13,000-foot Mt. Queen Mary in the St. Elias Range, Yukon Territory.

❝ My late husband, Bill Degenhardt, started climbing before such delicacies and conveniences as instant potatoes, dry milk, minute rice, and quick-cooking noodles were available. He used to tell of cooking dried beans on some of his early climbing expeditions—the kind of beans that require long soaking and hours of simmering to make them edible. He managed by soaking the beans in cold water overnight, boiling them over the breakfast fire, and then wrapping the hot kettle in newspapers and carefully setting it inside his sleeping bag to keep warm while the day's climb was in progress. When the climbers returned to camp, the beans were still warm, and soft enough to eat.

Most of my climbing-camp cooking was before the days of freeze-dried foods. I believed in keeping meals simple. A standard dinner menu was a one-pot stew, with a dessert of cookies, a cup of hot fruit-flavored gelatin dessert, and hot tea. It made an ideal combination to carry into high camp, to prepare quickly over a one-burner stove, and to eat while standing at a chilly viewpoint or crouched in a tent in a steady downpour. Other good one-pot stews can be made by cooking dehydrated or freeze-dried vegetables to taste, and mixing with either canned roast beef and instant mashed potatoes, or with canned boned chicken and instant rice. ❞

John Fitzgerald
ADIRONDACKS BARLEY SOUP

*Water, 1½ to 3 cups (use enough to
achieve desired thickness)*
*1 package oxtail or vegetable beef soup
mix*
*Vegetables, dehydrated or freeze-dried,
to taste*
*1 handful or more of quick-cooking
barley*

1 can meat (optional)
1 hunk cheese (optional)
1 gob butter or margarine (optional)
Pepper, lots, to taste
2 ounces sherry (optional)

*Mix water, soup, vegetables, and barley; bring to boil, and boil till ingredients are
tender, about 10 minutes. Add whatever you have in the way of meat, cheese, butter,
etc. Flavor with desired amount of pepper. For a gourmet touch, add 2 ounces of
sherry, which can be carried in a small vial. Vary amount of water according to
personal desires, but use enough to make a rich tasty soup. Serves 2.*

John Fitzgerald published *Wilderness Camping* in Scotia, a town just north
of Schenectady in east-central New York. The magazine, which catered to
the interests of backpackers, canoeists, cross-country skiers, and bicy-
clists, among others, merged with *Backpacker* magazine in 1979.

❝ I grew up in beautiful West Virginia, beside a river where I could either
canoe on the water or hike on the shores whenever I wished. I have enjoyed
cross-country skiing in the Rockies and Cascades, but I can also virtually ski
out my own back door in the Schenectady area, where deep snows and cold
temperatures are winter commonplaces.

As I stated in a magazine column a few years ago, I have always been a bit
smug about the relative closeness of the Adirondacks to my home—but I
have discovered even closer water routes. The streams don't flow through
the wilderness; but they are tree-bordered tricky routes that wind down old
glacial valleys, past farms, and often right along the railroad tracks. The
water is not drinkable (not yet, anyway). But on two successive weekends, I
saw from my canoe two does, a buck, and a fawn; a great blue heron, five
hawks, eight pairs of wild ducks, and other water birds; several assorted
turtles; many squirrels, chipmunks, and muskrats; and a great variety of
fish. This is the stuff that makes for a nice weekend on the water!

When it comes to cooking I lean toward simplicity and lots of quick-
cooking barley. It is sold in many supermarkets in my area. It cooks in about
ten minutes, compared with an hour or so for regular barley. ❞

Guy Gosselin
MULTITUDE-OF-SINS SAUCE

1 16-ounce can of tomatoes
1 package onion soup mix
1 fresh onion, chopped
3 to 4 slices processed American cheese
1 large pinch cinnamon
Salt and pepper to taste

Walnuts or almonds (optional)
Cornstarch or flour to thicken
Old porridge, bread, meat; or cooked
    rice, noodles, or instant mashed
    potatoes

*To tomatoes add soup mix; simmer. Dice up onion, and throw it into the pot along
with the cheese. Add flavorings and nuts. Mix cornstarch or flour into cold water to
make thin paste, and stir enough into the boiling mixture to thicken to near glacial
consistency. Serve sauce over leftovers to cover up a multitude of sins; or if you really
have 2 pots instead of only 1, serve sauce over rice, noodles, etc., prepared as directed
on package.*

Guy Gosselin, a lifelong resident of Gorham, New Hampshire spends
two weeks a month on the summit of Mt. Washington, the highest peak in
the White Mountains, where he is director of the Mount Washington Observatory.

❝ The observatory is a private nonprofit organization primarily devoted
to scientific research and educational endeavors such as the summit
museum. But it has had a lot to do with hikers and hiker safety over the
years, including search and rescue, particularly in winter. The peak's elevation is only 6288 feet, but the top is approximately 3000 feet above timberline
and lies in the path of three major tracks. It has some of the most severe and
rapidly changing weather known outside polar regions—the climate on top
is comparable to that of Labrador. Since records have been kept, its
maximum temperature has never exceeded 72° F, and the lowest was 47°
below zero. As much as forty-nine inches of snow have fallen in a single day,
and 566 inches in a year.

But it is the wind that gives Mt. Washington its claim to the world's worst
weather. Velocities in excess of 75 miles per hour—hurricane force—occur
on an average of 104 days a year; winds of 100 miles an hour are common in
winter and not unknown in summer. The mountain also holds the record for
observed surface winds—231 miles an hour in April 1934. There are few, if
any, other places in the world that have such high winds in combination
with below-zero temperatures. Besides that, the summit is swathed in
dense fog 60 percent of the time. No wonder hikers often find themselves in
trouble. ❞

Trudy Healy
CANYONLANDS HAM DINNER

2 to 3 cups water
1 1¼-ounce package freeze-dried ham
1 0.8-ounce package freeze-dried green
    beans

2 packages instant tomato or cream of
    mushroom soup
1 tablespoon dry minced onion

*Stir all ingredients together, using enough water for desired consistency when done.
Heat and cook till ingredients are tender and well blended. Serves 2.*

Trudy Healy grew up in the Black Forest of southwestern Germany. After
spending many years in the eastern United States, she and her husband,
George, now live in Sandy, Utah, near Salt Lake City. Trudy wrote *A
Climber's Guide to the Adirondacks* and for some years was editor or art editor
of various other mountain publications.

❝ I came by climbing naturally. My grandparents were alpinists and my
parents, hikers. My family took me to the highest summit in our region
when I was five. I was about ten when on a glacier for the first time, and as a
teenager in the Bavarian Alps made my first rock climbs with felt-soled(!)
klettershoes. I progressed to general mountaineering and technical climbing in the Alps, Dolomites, Colorado Rockies, Adirondacks, the Shawangunks in southeastern New York, and at Seneca Rock in West Virginia. I
have also been on trips to Peru, Ecuador, and Mexico. All six of our children,
now grown, are active in mountain sports.
In Utah, I have been active in a local mountain club as hiking director,
member of the ski-touring committee, and instructor in the club's avalanche
course. Although basically a mountaineer, I accept the Southwest desert
wholeheartedly. One recent October, my daughter Susan and I had been
trudging down Salt Creek in Canyonlands National Park in southeastern
Utah, mostly through deep loose sand along a jeep road in the canyon
bottom. Our camp for the night was on a high shelf under a protective
overhang. Soon after we had crawled into our bags, huddling close to the
rock wall, lightning began to flash and thunder to reverberate among the
canyon walls. Rain slashed down furiously. This went on all night. The roar
of churning water and tumbling rocks in the wash could only mean a flash
flood. When morning dawned, we stared down at our dry sandy route of
the day before—it was now a raging dark red torrent.
We hadn't slept much and were ready for a big breakfast, but our butane
stove wouldn't light. Wood gathering is not allowed there (everything was
wet anyway). We ate some gorp and left for a spectacular hike over the
mesas, in the brilliant sunshine and well-cleaned air. Every sandstone
depression was filled with rain-water reflecting the deep blue of the sky—
the fantastic Red Rock Desert of southern Utah, loaded with basins of pure,
sparkling, potable water! This sight alone was worth a million missed
breakfasts. ❞

Sibylle Hechtel
CAMP FOUR CURRY

1 to 3 cups water
½ to 1 cup bulgur
Onion, fresh or dry, chopped; or ½
    package onion soup mix
Indian curry powder
½ to 1 cup dry milk

1 6½-ounce can tuna
Dried fruit to taste (raisins, figs,
    apricots, or peaches)
Peanuts to taste
Coconut flakes

Heat water; add bulgur, and boil for about 10 minutes. Add onion, curry, dry milk, tuna, and fruit. Boil 5 or 10 minutes longer, or until bulgur is tender. Just before serving, stir in peanuts. Sprinkle coconut on top of individual servings. Regular brown rice may be substituted for the bulgur, but it takes longer to cook and doesn't taste as good. Serves 2.

Sibylle Hechtel is a biologist in the Division of Biology at the University of Michigan at Ann Arbor. She has done many difficult rock climbs, including ascents of Big Walls in Yosemite Valley above Camp Four.

❝ I was born in Stuttgart, Germany to mountaineering parents, Richard and Lisa Hechtel, who met while climbing. My father made many first ascents in Europe and has climbed extensively in the United States and in other regions.

Some of the Big Wall routes I have done in Yosemite are the South Face of Washington Column, the West Face of the Leaning Tower, and the Northwest Face of Half Dome. On El Capitan I did the Nose route in four days, the Salathe Wall in five, and the first all-woman ascent of the Triple Direct, with Beverly Johnson, in seven days. Elsewhere in the Sierra Nevada, I did the Southwest Face of Conness in about ten hours, and the first free one-day ascent of the East Face of Keeler Needle (the 14,240-foot summit just south of Mt. Whitney). I have done new routes on the North Face of Mt. Mitchell in Wyoming and on the West Face of Snowpatch Spire in the Bugaboos of British Columbia and have climbed Mexico's three highest volcanoes.

Multi-day climbs on Big Walls pose quite a weight problem. On the Triple Direct, Bev and I hauled the equivalent of our own weight—this included fifty-six pounds (seven gallons) of water, some forty pounds of climbing hardware and equipment, and of course food. On wall climbs we don't take stoves because of the weight. For breakfast we usually have granola, and during the day we just eat gorp, maybe a salami or tuna sandwich, and a couple of cans of fruit—peaches, mandarin oranges, apricots, or plums. ❞

Carolyn Hoffman
EASTERN TRAIL STEW

2 cups water
1 cup instant or minute rice
2 envelopes instant spring vegetable
*   soup*
Salt to taste

Large pinch parsley flakes (optional)
Canned seafood (6 ½-ounce can tuna,
*   7 ¾-ounce can salmon, or 1 or 2*
*   4 ½-ounce cans shrimp)*

Bring water to boil. Add rice, soup, and flavorings. Remove from heat (in cold weather or at high elevations, boil a few minutes first). Let stand about 10 minutes till rice is tender. Add fish and stir. Reheat if necessary. Serves 2.

Carolyn Hoffman of Dillsburg, Pennsylvania has hiked and backpacked for most of her life on forest and mountain trails in the eastern United States. She is author of a book on eastern Pennsylvania trails and is Pennsylvania coordinator for the International Backpackers Association (IBA) based in Lincoln Center, Maine. Carolyn was trek coordinator for the 3300-mile North Country Trail hike sponsored by the IBA in 1978.

❝ This eight-month hike focused on the proposal to include the largely unbuilt North Country Trail in the National Scenic Trails System. On March 5, 1978, five of us set out from Crown Point in northwestern New York, bound for Four Bears Memorial Park in western North Dakota. We traveled through seven states and averaged about fourteen miles a day.

We traversed New York State and crossed the northwest corner of Pennsylvania. When we reached Ohio we had lost so much time that we traveled partway by bicycle. We went southwest and then westward through Ohio, generally following the course of the Ohio River, and then northward to Michigan. We walked north through Michigan to Lake Superior, then westward across northern Michigan, Wisconsin, and central Minnesota. We crossed North Dakota and on October 13 arrived at Four Bears. Only two of us—Lou Ann Fellows from El Mesa, California and I—reached our goal.

The route is not primarily wilderness oriented. We passed through a variety of ecological areas, including the Adirondacks, a section beside the Erie Canal, farmlands, and grasslands (or prairies). We followed existing trails, railroads, snowmobile trails, logging roads, streams, the shorelines of lakes—anything that fell within the ten-mile proposed corridor for the future trail. We planned a combination of fresh and freeze-dried foods, part 'drop-shipped' to us at post offices en route and part purchased at local stores. The North Country Trail was officially approved by President Carter on March 5, 1980, the second anniversary of our start. ❞

Thomas F. Hornbein
UNMENTIONABLE BREW

4 cups water
1 to 2 packages soup mix (any flavor or combination)
Freeze-dried vegetables (peas, carrots, etc., any amount)
Dry minced onion, bean sprouts, etc., to taste
Freeze-dried hamburger, broken up (or other freeze-dried meat to taste)
Salt, pepper, curry, etc., to taste
Instant or minute rice, instant mashed potatoes, etc. (optional)

Put water on to heat. Add soup, vegetables, and meat in any flavor, combination, or amount. Add seasonings listed or a few other exotic condiments. At the stage of cooking that seems indicated by package directions or experience, enrich the brew (if desired) with rice, a small quantum of instant mashed potatoes, or other such stuff. The end result is a large molten mass of material anywhere between a moderately thick soup to something that would require an ice axe to disarticulate.

Thomas F. Hornbein, M.D. of Bellevue, Washington, with Willi Unsoeld, ascended the unclimbed West Ridge of Mt. Everest and descended to the South Col on May 22, 1963, thus accomplishing a new route and the first traverse of the world's highest peak. The 1963 American Everest Expedition also placed four men on the summit via the South Col: James Whittaker and Nawang Gombu on May 1, and Barry Bishop and Luther Jerstad on May 22. Dr. Hornbein was in charge of expedition oxygen equipment. *Everest: The West Ridge,* by Dr. Hornbein, documents the new route and the traverse of the 29,028-foot Himalayan peak.

❝ I have been active in mountaineering since 1944, particularly in the western United States. In 1957 I was on an expedition to then-unclimbed Mt. Huntington in the Alaska Range (the 12,240-foot peak remained unclimbed until 1964 when the first ascent was made by a French party led by Lionel Terray). In 1960 I was on the American expedition to the Karakoram that made the first ascent of 25,660-foot Masherbrum—Willi Unsoeld and George I. Bell climbed it July 6, and Nick Clinch and Jawed Akhter July 8.

I don't really have much in the way of culinary input, because my major single article of diet in the mountains is a rather large pot of this Unmentionable Brew. One beauty of this particular concoction is the fact that if you make enough at dinnertime, then all you have to do is heat the pot next morning and have more of same before taking off. ❞

Jerry Johnson
ALASKA GLOP

3 to 4 cups water
Noodles or rice (consult package directions for amount needed for desired bulk)
Hard sausage, cut up (or freeze-dried meat)
Freeze-dried vegetables to taste
Dry onion, minced or chopped
1 package gravy mix (any flavor)
Salt, pepper, oregano, thyme (to taste)
Margarine
Cheese, chopped or slivered
Dried egg mix or freeze-dried eggs

Heat water. Add noodles or rice (if instant or minute rice is used, add toward end of cooking period). Add meat, vegetables, gravy mix, flavorings, and margarine. Boil till all ingredients are tender; stir occasionally to keep mix from sticking to bottom of pot. Shortly before serving stir in enough cheese and powdered egg to thicken. Serves 2.

Jerry Johnson of Fairbanks, Alaska lived and attended college in Alaska for some years and later majored in avalanche mechanics at the University of Washington. While working on his doctorate, he split his time between Mt. Baker and Washington Pass in the North Cascades, and the Rogers Pass avalanche research station in British Columbia, studying various aspects of snow avalanches and their control.

❝ This glop really sticks to the ribs. The noodles or rice provide the bulk. The eggs and cheese thicken it and, with the margarine, turn it into a gourmet meal. Sausage is delicious and provides some of the extra fat needed in cold climates. The desire for fat in the diet determines the amount of margarine used. On climbs longer than one-and-a-half or two weeks, it isn't uncommon for two people to need up to a quarter of a pound per meal. We used to enjoy this glop on Alaska climbing trips, and I still use it on my mountain outings in the Pacific Northwest. ❞

Celia Hunter and Ginny Wood
TUNDRA TREK GLOP

Freeze-dried vegetables (to taste)
Freeze-dried meat (chicken, ham, or beef)
3 to 4 cups water
Noodles or rice (instant or regular)

Butter or margarine
1 package sauce mix (spaghetti, chili, hollandaise, sour cream, mushroom, etc., to taste)

Soak freeze-dried vegetables and meat together in water. Meanwhile heat water, and boil noodles or rice. Heat vegetables, meat, and sauce together till soft. Add the vegetable-meat-sauce mixture to noodles or rice. Bring to boil. Instant mashed potatoes may be substituted for noodles or rice, but should be added toward end of cooking period in amount needed for desired thickness. Serves 2 to 3.

From 1952 to 1975, Ginny Wood and Celia Hunter operated a wilderness resort and guide service located just outside the north boundary of Mount McKinley National Park (now Denali National Park), twenty-five air miles from Mt. McKinley. Cozy overnight facilities were provided in cabins or tents, and backpackers were guided into the park for hiking, camping, and photography. Celia and Ginny now share a large log house in Dogpatch, Alaska, nine miles northwest of Fairbanks.

Celia was interim executive director of the Wilderness Society in Washington, D.C. from 1976 to 1978, when she returned to Alaska. At that time she began writing a weekly environmental column in the Fairbanks Daily News Miner. Since June 1980 she has edited a monthly column, "This Our Land," in Alaska magazine. She helped found and is chairman of the Board of Trustees of the Alaska Conservation Foundation, the first public interest group in Alaska, which raises money for Alaskan conservation groups.

❝ Ginny and I discovered Alaska's beauty when we ferried two planes up the Alcan Highway after World War II. After we started our guide service, I took care of the camp and business, and Ginny guided and cooked for the backpacking trips. Above all other recollections I treasure the feeling of self-reliance, the sense of independence, and the ability to cope with and overcome the barriers or problems of natural circumstances. ❞

Ginny is still a professional guide in Alaska. From June to early September she takes small groups to remote areas such as the Brooks Range, the Gates of the Arctic region, and the Arctic National Wildlife Refuge.

❝ Groups are flown in. Our summers produce all sorts of weather, from 80° to blizzards. The Alaskan tundra is fragile. On my 'Tundra Treks' I limit the number to eight, and in some delicate areas to no more than three or four, including the leader, to minimize the impact. (I encourage tennis shoes or moccasins around camp in the evening, but not for walking on scree, permafrost, boulders, snowfields, etc.)**99**

Mrs. F.D. (Harriet) Mack
NORTH STAR GINGER DUMPLINGS

2 ½ cups water
4 ounces dried apples
Sugar to taste

½ of a 14-ounce gingerbread mix
Just enough water to make a stiff
dough (about ¼ cup)

Cook dried apples with water and sugar till they are tender. Make a stiff (not runny) batter by combining the gingerbread mix with about half the water called for on the box for the proportion of mix used. Make sure applesauce is wet enough so it won't scorch during further cooking. With a large spoon drop globs of dough onto the bubbling applesauce. Place lid tightly over pot, and simmer for about half an hour (it may take longer at a high elevation). Dumplings rise in the steam, so don't peek under the lid until the specified time has passed. Serve as is, or add anything else you have such as nuts, shaved chocolate, berries, or canned fruit.

The late Mrs. F.D. (Harriet) Mack—"Rick" to her friends—lived in Sunnyside, Washington before her death in 1980. Mrs. Mack started her hiking career more than sixty years ago by helping her husband with Boy Scout affairs. In the years following her first outings, she hiked alpine trails in the Cascades, Olympics, Sierra Nevada, Rockies, and the Swiss Alps; among the fjords of Norway; in the Himalayas of Nepal; and in Patagonia.

❝ A few years ago I figured out that for fifty years I averaged about 350 miles a year of backpacking, with a total of some 17,500 miles; and I spent at least a thousand nights on the ground in a sleeping bag. I took up skiing after I became a grandmother, and thereafter skied extensively in the North Cascades and elsewhere.

I invented Ginger Dumplings in the late 1940's, when I was ski touring with friends in the North Cascades west of Lake Chelan. For five weeks we had skied, backpacked, and camped out nightly on deep snow. But none of us was quite ready to end our trip, even though food supplies had dwindled to a package of gingerbread mix and a sack of dried apples. Nobody was sure what to do with that combination. But I felt I would think of something, so I told the others to start the fire and make camp while I got the dinner. The result was far more delectable than some of the things we had mixed together according to plan. I named the recipe after North Star Mountain opposite our campsite. ❞

J. Alex Maxwell
GLUE STEW

3 to 4 cups water
Soup mix, any flavor
Dried vegetables to taste (or freeze-dried vegetables)
1 12-ounce can corned beef; or jerky (or freeze-dried meat)
Salt, curry, or other strong flavorings to punch up taste

Reconstitute dried vegetables as time and type permit. Boil everything together. (For a truly traditional old-time flavor, give sufficient inattention to assure generous portions being scorched on the bottom of the pan.) When ingredients are reasonably tender (and all rodents for half a mile around have been spooked with its nutritious permeating odor), this glutinous glue is ready to eat.

J. Alex (Lex) Maxwell of Yakima, Washington is a pioneer climber, backpacker, and skier, and a leader in Washington State mountain rescue work. Lex put up new routes on Mt. Adams, Mt. Stuart, Ingalls Peak, Kloochman Rock, and elsewhere in the Cascades. Besides climbing all the major peaks in the Cascades of Washington and Oregon, he has made ascents in the St. Elias Range in Alaska, in the Bugaboos of British Columbia, and of 17,887-foot Popocatepetl in Mexico.

❝ Glue Stew is a formula obtained in the pharmacy of the packsack. The original ingredients date back to the days of dehydrated foods, which were slow to reconstitute compared with modern freeze-dried varieties. This brew wasn't too bad in a base camp because you could let the ingredients soak overnight; but when you were on the move and had limited cooking time, the dried foods were generally pretty tasteless, and the outcome sometimes pretty awful.

A version I particularly remember was dished up in the North Cascades. Bob McCall, Bob Swenson, my wife, Mary, and I came down off Clark Mountain and were preparing our leave-taking meal in a beautiful but rainy meadow. We fellows were huddled under our ponchos as we tossed remnants of our food into one last mixture that Bob Swenson was stirring with a stick. Mary joined us, looked suspiciously at our concoction, and said, 'What kind of soup is that?' Just then, a big green beetle nose-dived into the soup with an audible plop. Without losing a stroke of his stirring, Swenson flatly stated, 'This is split beetle soup.' ❞

Faye Ogilvie
GOLDMEYER DUMPLINGS

1 cup flour
1 ½ teaspoon baking powder
1 tablespoon freeze-dried eggs or dried egg mix
2 tablespoons dry milk
½ teaspoon poultry seasoning or onion powder
½ teaspoon salt
1 package freeze-dried vegetable stew
Meat to taste (freeze-dried, canned, or 2-ounce meat bar)
Boiling water to total 3 cups in pot before adding dumplings
½ cup cold water
2 tablespoons oil or melted fat

At home, mix together the flour, baking powder, egg mix, dry milk, seasoning, and salt. Carry this mix in a tightly sealed plastic bag. In camp, prepare the freeze-dried vegetables as directed on package; add meat, and boil till stew is almost done. Check to make sure the liquid in pot totals approximately 3 cups. Now stir the dry dumpling mix with ½ cup cold water and 2 tablespoons oil or melted fat. Drop dough by teaspoonfuls into the boiling stew. Cover tightly. Without raising lid, simmer for 15 to 20 minutes. Serve at once. Serves 2.

Faye Ogilvie lives in Seattle, Washington. Her husband, Ellis, died in November 1979. Faye has served as secretary of the Federation of Outdoor Clubs and is active in conservation work as well as backpacking.

❝ I'm not really famed for my ability as a trail cook—but at least once, a recipe of mine struck the right spot. Ellis and I were finishing a circle trip from Salmon la Sac (east of the Cascade Crest), over Dutch Miller Gap down to Goldmeyer Hot Springs, and up the Rock Creek Trail to Snow Lake, en route to catching a bus at Snoqualmie Pass. Ellis was taking antibiotics for what the doctor called 'walking pneumonia.' After hiking from Hardscrabble Creek to Rock Creek, he was feeling low. It was there that I made my hit with Goldmeyer Dumplings. Brings back the spring. ❞

Leigh Ortenburger
MOUNTAIN HOOSH

Butter or margarine
6 to 8 ounces meat (canned ham
  chunks, corned beef, chicken,
  etc.; or frankfurters; or equivalent
  amount in freeze-dried meat)
2 to 4 cups water
Soup mix (optional)
Vegetables, dried or freeze-dried
  (optional)

2 bouillon cubes
Pepper (plenty)
Herbs and spices to taste
Rice (minute or instant) or instant
  mashed potatoes
Cheese, cut up or shredded

Melt butter in pan; add meat, and cook it thoroughly in butter. Add water. Start out with a little less than you expect to need, so the hoosh won't be too soupy after adding rice or potatoes. Bring to boil. Add vegetables and/or soup mix, and cook till nearly done. Add bouillon cubes and flavorings. Add rice or potatoes, following package directions. Allow extra cooking time at high elevations. Add cheese last; stir till it is melted to prevent cheese from settling to the bottom and scorching. Immediately remove pot from heat. Serves 2 to 4. (The word hoosh *was used on Captain Robert Scott's 1911-1912 South Pole expedition when he had to cook pony meat after all other available food had been used up.)*

Leigh Ortenburger of Palo Alto, California began climbing in 1948. He guided and made first ascents in the Tetons and wrote *A Climber's Guide to the Teton Range*. He was on an expedition to Makalu in Nepal in 1961 and has climbed extensively in South America.

❝ Between 1952 and 1977 I was on seven expeditions in the Cordillera Blanca of the Peruvian Andes. I climbed twenty-five peaks, all over 6000 meters (19,500 feet) in elevation. These climbs included one first ascent, fifteen second ascents, and six new routes—among them, new routes on Huascarán (22,205 feet), Huandoy (20,981 feet), and Chacraraju (20,052 feet).

My favorite mountain is the Grand Teton, which I have climbed seventy times. In 1951 Dick Irvin, John Mowat, Nick Clinch, and I had climbed the East Ridge of the Grand. We had to spend the night at the Lower Saddle and ran out of food. Next morning, though rather hungry, we declined Nick's emergency ration of war-surplus pemmican, which we considered nearly inedible. Just before dropping into the couloir leading down toward the Teton Glacier, we decided to scale two pinnacles which we thought might be unclimbed. That meant we needed a can for a summit note, so had to eat the pemmican to liberate the can. Clinch passed the stuff around, and I said, 'No, thank you.' Clinch exploded, 'You'll eat your fair share!' As a result, in my Teton guidebook, I provided unofficial names for the two pinnacles we climbed: Pemmican Pillar and Fairshare Tower. ❞

Greg Rayer
POTATO-CHEESE SOUP

4 cups water
1 tablespoon oil or butter
½ cup instant mashed potatoes
½ cup dry milk
4 tablespoons flour
1 tablespoon wheat germ

1 tablespoon dry onion, minced
1 teaspoon parsley flakes
½ teaspoon salt (or to taste)
½ pound cheese (grated Parmesan, or
    cheddar cut into chunks)

Put all ingredients except cheese into cold water. Stir well. Bring to boil while stirring continuously. Simmer from 5 to 10 minutes, and stir from time to time. Remove from heat, add cheese, stir well. Serves 2.

Greg Rayer of Lexington, Kentucky is a backpacker whose work is primarily with young teenage boys.

❞ As a teacher of children with emotional and behavioral problems, I am always looking for ways to turn kids on to learning in a meaningful and realistic fashion. The central Kentucky Re-Ed Program, run by the Kentucky Department for Human Resources in the seventeen-county Bluegrass Region, is a short-term residential program that aids children who have not been able to make it in their homes, schools, and communities.

The International Backpackers Association 'Project One for the Trail' seemed to be a perfect medium to help in this work. We set up a training program where each boy learned about the beauty of the outdoors and the companionship and joys of the trail, and became competent in the basic skills of camping, map reading, first aid, and cooking. The students gleaned recipes from various sources, bought the ingredients needed, tried out the dishes, and decided which they wanted to take on their backpack, canoe, and caving trips.

Our group, which we dubbed the Rangers, went on several day hikes, tested equipment, and developed a tremendous group spirit. On two extended trips in one recent year, they cleaned up over a hundred campsites, marked several trails, and built more than two miles of a north-south trail that will eventually run from Morehead in northeast Kentucky south to the Tennessee border. ❞

Bill Shepard
SIERRA SOUP

1 5-ounce box brown and wild rice
1¾ to 2 cups water
1 envelope instant green pea soup,
    combined with scant ½ cup
    water

Croutons (optional)
Slivered almonds (optional)
Fresh onions, chopped and fried in
    butter (optional)
Other condiments, to taste

Prepare rice, using 1¾ to 2 cups water, according to directions on package (allow 20 to 30 minutes for cooking). Stir up the pea soup with a scant ½ cup of water (about half the amount called for on the package). Combine soup and rice. This makes a hearty meal in itself. It is even better with the addition of croutons, almonds, onions, etc. Serves 2.

Bill Shepard, a backpacker from Quincy, California is a free-lance writer-editor-photographer. He writes backpacking articles and has edited a trade paper for private campground owners. He has been editor of *Wild Country*, a national monthly newsletter for wilderness campers, and of *Trail Camping Magazine* and *Camping Guide Magazine*, all of which are now out of publication. Bill presently is editor of *California Horse Review Magazine*.

❝ In the late 1960's I helped start a family backpack group that still makes one hike a year. It started out with the usual dehydrated foods, but gradually deteriorated into gourmet cooking. As these hikes are rarely longer than two to four miles, we can carry such things as steaks, melons, fresh strawberries, and champagne.

On my own mountain outings, my menu is considerably more Spartan. Breakfast is usually instant oatmeal in a cup, followed by hot chocolate; lunch may be crackers with peanut butter and honey; and dinner something freeze-dried. I get by with just a teakettle for heating water. To simplify meals still further, I have tried hiking with cold rations, but this has only been moderately successful.

Over the years I have put up with a good many remarks about my frugal meals—especially about my cup-of-oatmeal breakfasts. So when planning meals for one snow backpack in the Sierra, I decided to surprise my two partners. I took Canadian bacon and packed six eggs in sawdust in a milk carton—very inconvenient in the pack. Next morning, as we hunkered over a little fire in the chill, I nonchalantly fried the bacon, served it, and asked, 'How do you like your eggs?' I had expected an enthusiastic reply, but one of my partners exhibited a strange lack of appreciation for my efforts. He finally said, 'You know, I was pretty cold early this morning before we got up, and I really had my mind set on a cup of hot oatmeal.' ❞

John Simac
SCHURMAN HUT HAM-AND-RICE

2 ¼ cups water
7-ounce box minute or instant rice
2 ounces freeze-dried peas
6 ¾-ounce can ham chunks or equivalent in freeze-dried ham
Flavorings to taste

Bring water to boil. Add rice and peas. Simmer for 3 minutes, stirring to prevent sticking; add more water if needed. If freeze-dried ham is used, reconstitute according to package directions. Add ham to rice-pea mixture, reheat (stirring well), and serve. Serves 2.

John Simac of Tacoma, Washington has climbed Mt. McKinley and was on the first official winter ascent of Mt. Rainier in 1965. His many contributions in the field of mountain rescue work include developing a backpackable hydraulic winch and helping develop the "storm kit" produced by the Tacoma Mountain Rescue Unit.

John Simac was one of the prime builders of Schurman Hut, constructed between 1958 and 1962 at the base of Steamboat Prow on the north side of Mt. Rainier. The hut, at 9500 feet elevation and about 5000 feet above the roadhead, serves not only as a high camp for climbers ascending the peak by the Emmons Glacier, but also as an emergency shelter in case of storm or accident. During the construction period, Simac climbed to this site at least 135 times, to carry materials and assist in building the shelter.

❮❮ Late one year, with winter approaching, there were still some heavy loads to be carried up the glacier to the hut site. Our days were so full and time so short that we often brought a good, nourishing, home-cooked stew that could just be heated up for dinner. One evening, when the weather was extremely cold, our non-pump-type stove kept going out—very trying to our patience. At long last, the stew began to simmer. Holding the pot lid in one hand and a spoon in the other, with a flashlight tucked between chin and chest so I could see into the pot, I began to stir. The flashlight slipped and fell into the stew. The pot became top-heavy and tipped over—and the entire dinner spilled over onto the pumice. All those cold, tired, hungry, hard-working climbers had to go to bed without. ❯❯

Bob and Ira Spring
QUICK MOUNTAIN GLOP

3 to 4 cups water
1 package vegetable soup mix
Meat (jar chipped beef, small can corned beef, or other meat)
Instant mashed potatoes

Heat water, add soup mix, and cook till done, about 20 minutes. Turn off heat and add meat. Stir in enough potato to achieve desired consistency and to satisfy appetites. Serve at once. Serves 2 to 4. A good variation is to add instant or minute rice (instead of potato) to the soup. Cook until almost done (be careful not to burn the rice), and remove from heat. Stir in a small can of tuna or boned chicken. Cover, and let stand a few more minutes. The longer it stands, the more tender the rice; but remember, it cools quickly.

Bob and Ira Spring of Edmonds, Washington are photographers whose specialty—mountain, scenic, historic, cultural, and travel photography—has taken them and their families to many parts of the world. "Photos by Bob and Ira Spring" have appeared since the 1940's in national magazines, outdoor and conservation publications, and regional newspapers. The Spring brothers have taken pictures in Japan, Norway, Russia, and Europe—and especially in Alaska and their native Pacific Northwest.

Ira says that because he carries so much camera equipment, there isn't much space left for food, nor much time for cooking. He shops at the supermarket (he says freeze-dried foods are fine but they cost too much for daily use). His meals must be quick and simple; they may be monotonous—but the scenery outside his tent seldom is.

❝ My most memorable experience with food was running out of it. Two other climbers and I were within sight of civilization after a two-week trek on the Juneau Icefield. Juneau was so close that we could see cars moving on the streets below. There was no question, we would be down there the next morning for breakfast. At what should have been our last camp, we had a big meal of the remaining food and squandered the rest of our gas drying socks. All that was left were six prunes, a jar of jam, two raisins, and an empty stove. However, that night it rained and turned cold, and the small cliff we had to descend was solid ice. It took all day to go a quarter-mile and we were stuck out another night, this time without heat to melt snow. We divided the prunes, two for each person, and made a large pot of ice cream with jam and snow. We couldn't figure out how to divide the two raisins three ways, so we flipped for them and I won both. ❞

Constance Stallings
CATSKILLS GLOP

1 teaspoon salt
4 cups water
7¼-ounce package macaroni and
    cheese dinner

¼ cup dry milk
2 tablespoons parsley flakes
1 6½-ounce can tuna or 5-ounce can
    boned chicken

Add salt to water, and bring to a full boil. Add macaroni, and cook 8 to 10 minutes or until done; stir as needed. Drain out water, taking care not to drain out macaroni as well. Stir in the cheese packaged with the macaroni dinner. Add milk, parsley, and fish or meat. Put back on heat to melt cheese, and stir thoroughly. If there are any nuts left over from the day's gorp supply, chop them up and throw in for interest. Serves 2 to 4.

Constance (Connie) Stallings of Brooklyn, New York is publications editor for the National Audubon Society and president of East Woods Press, a regional publishing company. She is coauthor of *Ecotactics* and *Hiker's Guide to the Smokies*. Additionally, she has edited *Canoeing the Jersey Pine Barrens*, *John Muir's Longest Walk*, and hiking guides for Virginia, the Catskill Mountains, and the Rocky Mountains.

❞ I started hiking at about age seven, when my father was director of a boys' camp in Vermont. My sister and I often went along on their hikes. We covered portions of Vermont's Long Trail, not then widely known. The Long Trail, patterned after the Appalachian Trail, stretches from Vermont's southern border to its northern border—the Canadian border—a distance of more than 150 airline miles.

My favorite hiking area is the Catskills in southeastern New York State. These mountains lie west of the Hudson, about a two-and-a-half hour drive north from New York City, a good place for day hikes. I also love to snowshoe, and for this reason winter is perhaps my favorite season. ❞

Thomas Winnett
SHRIMP SIERRA

1 package leek or cream of onion soup mix	*¼ teaspoon parsley flakes*
3 cups water	*¼ teaspoon dried celery*
1 small package dried shrimp (1 or more ounces to taste), cut up	*¼ teaspoon dry mustard*
¼ cup freeze-dried mushrooms	*¼ teaspoon monosodium glutamate*
¼ cup mixed dried vegetables	*⅛ teaspoon white pepper*
	¾ teaspoon salt
	1 cup minute or instant rice

Put the soup mix into the pot, and add water a cup at a time; stir after each addition until the mixture is smooth and free of lumps. Add the shrimp, vegetables, herbs, and seasonings. Bring to a boil. Add the rice, partly cover, and allow to boil slowly for 5 to 7 minutes, or until rice is absorbed into liquid. Stir frequently till done. Serves 2.

Thomas Winnett of Berkeley, California has been going into the High Sierra with pack and fishing rod since 1936 — and in the process has accumulated and recorded a fund of backpacking information. He is the author of *Backpacking Basics* and of numerous trail guides covering areas in the Sierra Nevada and in the Pacific Northwest. In addition, he has edited and published many other trail guides under the imprint of the Wilderness Press. He is a life member of the Sierra Club and has served as vice-president of the California Wilderness Foundation.

❝ I am a strong advocate of wilderness and have worked to save the world's wild places. One of the most unusual incidents I remember about food happened a few years ago when my son Jason went ice fishing without a hook and line. It was in late October, near Tioga Pass, at 10,500 feet elevation in the Sierra Nevada. A small stream running through a meadow, Parker Pass Creek, was frozen over with about a quarter-inch of ice. Jason thought he spied some trout under the ice. He broke the ice and removed several chunks of it to give himself working room. Then he put his arm into the icy water up to his shoulder and kept feeling around under the banks. He finally brought out a twelve-inch trout, handed it to me, and put his arm back in the water. In a moment he brought out the first fish's twin. After photographing the event, I put the trout in my pack to grill for dinner. ❞

Frying Pan Foods

"Yes, you seem to have packed the eggs well enough...."

Anni Grasegger
EMPEROR'S SCRAMBLED PANCAKES

1 cup sifted all-purpose flour	1 cup milk (reconstituted dry)
1 tablespoon sugar	½ cup (¼-pound stick) butter (NOT
¼ teaspoon salt	margarine)
4 eggs, beaten	Sugar to use when serving

Combine flour, sugar, and salt in bowl or saucepan. Make a well in center of dry ingredients, and add eggs and milk. Beat until batter is smooth. Melt butter in frying pan, add the batter all at once, and cook until lightly browned on bottom. Turn over with spatula, as for scrambled eggs — the pancake will break into pieces. Continue to cook until the other side is lightly browned but the pancake is still moist. Serve sprinkled with sugar. It is delicious with applesauce on the side and a cup of hot, Italian style, orange-flavored instant coffee beverage. The German name for these pancakes is Kaiser Schmarren. *Serves 2.*

Anni Grasegger of Seattle, Washington was born and grew up in Garmisch-Partenkirchen in the foothills of the Bavarian Alps.

❝ I learned to ski in kindergarten, as did all my friends. I climbed Germany's highest mountain, the 9700-foot Zugspitze, for the first time when I was eleven. Since then, I have been in love with the outdoors. In 1953, after doing photographic work for fourteen years in my hometown, I emigrated to Seattle, where I am a lab technician specializing in color reproduction. Photography—and discovering the infinite beauty of the Pacific Northwest on foot and with my camera—are my main hobbies.

I particularly enjoy hiking in the Cascades. My favorite spot is Snow Lake, north of Snoqualmie Pass, as it reminds me so much of the lakes I know in the Bavarian Alps. I return fairly often to Bavaria. In the Bavarian Alps hiking means having, at all times, a *Hütte* (mountain lodge) as home base for shelter and meals. Like everywhere else, soups are the basic dishes. Lentil soup and green pea soup, with one of the many delicious Bavarian sausages, are favorites. Here, Bavarian sausage can be replaced by cocktail sausages available in glass jars. A popular trail snack in Germany is called *Studentenfutter*—named after university students who had to put together an inexpensive and readily available trail food. Usual ingredients are nuts, raisins, and chocolate, with the addition of dried fruits such as apples, pears, or peaches. ❞

Charles D. Hessey
LYMAN LAKE HOTCAKES

1 cup flour
⅔ cup buckwheat pancake mix
2 teaspoons baking powder
3 teaspoons sugar
½ teaspoon salt
Wheat germ to taste (optional)
1½ cups milk (more or less for thinner
    or thicker batter)

1 to 2 tablespoons oil or melted
    shortening
1 egg (optional)
Fat or oil for frying
Syrup (preferably made with wild
    blueberries, sugar, and water)

At home, sift flour, pancake mix, baking powder, sugar, and salt together 5 times. Add wheat germ. Pack in plastic bag. In camp, stir milk, shortening, and egg into dry mix. Fry hotcakes in greased skillet. Serves 2. The best syrup is made from wild blueberries or huckleberries cooked with sugar and water, and served hot.

Charles D. (Chuck) Hessey of Naches, Washington was camping, fishing, backpacking, and skiing in the North Cascades before World War II. After the war he made numerous cross-country ski treks from Holden, west of Lake Chelan, to a shelter cabin eight miles away at Lyman Lake (now in the Glacier Peak Wilderness Area). Chuck spent long periods at the cabin and left a log of weather observations and philosophy, which inspired those at the mining camp above Holden to give him the title "Lyman Lake Philosopher." Chuck and his wife, Marion, have contributed much toward preserving the North Cascades Wilderness—in part through Chuck's wildlife films.

❝ During my service with the United States Army in India, I had the experience—rare for an American—of skiing in the Vale of Kashmir. I had joined the Ski Club of India and was able to enjoy a ten-day ski outing at the Killenmarg hut at Gulmarg, then a British Air Force rest camp at over 10,000 feet elevation on the slopes of Mt. Apharwat. It was wonderful for a mountain-starved soldier from the Pacific Northwest. Conditions were similar to winter conditions on North Star Mountain near Lyman Lake. But there were some differences.

We were taken to the resort by lorry, with our personal possessions in dunnage bags. Our food supply was largely C rations, supplemented by tea, eggs, and brown sugar from a local bazaar. We rented boots and skis in Srinagar. From there we were transported by truck to the base of Apharwat. There we hired porters, who were barefoot except for sandals, to carry our gear to Killenmarg. They were the Indian version of a ski lift—supplemented by donkeys. Aided by our porters, we rode the donkeys up and skied down! ❞

Lute Jerstad
ULTRA EGGS

2 fresh eggs
Dried eggs to equal 2 fresh eggs
Chopped ham (canned chunks, or
    freeze-dried)

Green pepper, chopped (fresh or dried)
Salt and pepper to taste
Tabasco sauce to taste (a little)
Butter or margarine

Beat fresh eggs lightly. Add dried eggs reconstituted according to package directions. Add ham (if freeze-dried, reconstitute first as directed). Add seasonings. Melt fat in pan over low heat and pour in egg mixture. Stir gently, till done. Serve with orange flavor instant drink, cinnamon toast, and hot beverage for a delicious breakfast. Serves 2.

Luther (Lute) Jerstad of Portland, Oregon was one of the first four Americans to climb Mt. Everest, in 1963. He has also climbed extensively in the western United States, Alaska, the Yukon Territory, the Alps, the Cordillera Blanca of Peru, and the Himalaya. He is the author of *Everest Diary* and has written articles for assorted outdoor publications. Lute is head of a guide service now in its second decade of offering mountain and river wilderness trips.

❝ In the late 1970's we were the first to make runs on the Upper Ganges in northern India. The Bhagerathi branch provided some 120 miles of extremely wild water; the Alaknonda branch, another first run, was made with a TV crew. In the 1970's also we conducted a therapy and adventure program for mental patients. In the Pacific Northwest we provide instruction in rock, snow, and ice climbing, and trips by river, horseback, and backpack.

Some years ago, with Dick McGowan and Pete Schoening, I organized the first of the now numerous mountaineering seminars. The food for our seminars was largely provided by Frank and Lydia Bell, who used to own an inn at an Oregon ski area. They made up and froze large batches of spaghetti, chili, etc., for dinners at our Eliot Glacier base camp on Mt. Hood. The Bells also provided us with fresh salads from their large garden. One summer they talked our guides into serving goat milk to our clients without forewarning. The clients' screams of protest are still echoing in the canyons and craters of Mt. Hood. Goat milk was immediately stricken from our menus! ❞

Tim Kneeland
ALPINE UMPSKI

Potato (1 large fresh; or equivalent amount of frozen,
*   freeze-dried, or precooked dehydrated hashed brown)*
Butter, margarine, or oil
Bacon or sausage, cut up
Onion to taste (fresh or dry)
2 to 4 eggs (fresh or reconstituted dried)
Salt, pepper, and spices to taste

Pare and slice fresh potato, thaw frozen, or reconstitute dried potato as directed on package. Melt fat in frying pan, or pour in oil. Add potato, meat, and onion. Fry and stir. Beat (or reconstitute) eggs, and pour them over the other ingredients. Cook in pan till the eggs reach the desired consistency—wet or dry. Add appropriate spices. Serves 2.

Tim Kneeland of Minneapolis, Minnesota has taught outdoor recreation and survival skills since the mid-1960's in the Pacific Northwest and in the Minnesota area. He attended the University of Minnesota for an advanced degree in Recreation and Park Administration. Tim is training director for a Minnesota conservation organization that offers courses which include an introduction to winter hiking, snowshoeing, camping, cross-country skiing, coping with cold weather problems, and the psychology and physiology of Minnesota winter living.

❝ People often show a great deal of ignorance about how to live in harmony with the outdoors. I have a few hints that may prove helpful in summer and winter backpacking and outdoor cooking. Use a stove, not a fire, especially in alpine and subalpine regions and heavily used areas. Insulate the stove from cold or wet ground by setting it on a closed-cell foam pad or even a folded towel. Try out food you plan to take on a trip before you leave home. For just a weekend, fresh food or almost anything else is suitable. I have sometimes frozen a steak and transported it in a sealed plastic bag wrapped in a towel. It will keep cool for the first or second night out. To keep water cold in summer, freeze your filled canteen or water bottle before a trip; it will thaw slowly and give a steady supply of cold water. To keep it insulated from heat—or cold—wrap it in a wool sock (one you know the history of), or in a piece of closed-cell foam. In cold weather, sleeping with your canteen will keep it from freezing; or bury it in a snowbank.

Always consider your impact on the environment. Pack out all food wastes if they can't be burned. If other users are looking for solitude, take great care to blend with your environment, both visually and audibly. Remember that you can either enhance or dilute other wild land users' experiences. ❞

'I was here five years ago. It's the most gorgeous spot I've ever seen."

Ron Langevin
CANADA OMELET

½ can back bacon ("Canadian" bacon
   in the United States)
Dried egg equal to 6 eggs

1 envelope onion soup mix
Hot water, small amount
¼ pound cheddar cheese, cubed

Fry bacon and cut into small chunks. Reconstitute dried eggs as per package directions. Put the onion soup mix into a cup, and pour in just enough hot water to soften. Add eggs, moistened soup mix, and cheese cubes to the bacon chunks in the frying pan. Fry up the whole lot, stirring as necessary. (Stand back! You may be trampled by climbers or bears, depending on which gets there first.) Serves 2 or 3.

Ron Langevin of Banff, Alberta is a longtime mountaineer and a former forestry and national parks officer. Ron and his family live in a log house they built in the late 1970's after he left his park work.

❝ I have been a warden at Jasper National Park, park supervisor at Mount Robson Provincial Park, and in charge of campgrounds at Banff National Park. My personal interests have been mountaineering and photography, as well as travel to various mountain regions. I have been on two expeditions. One was to a 22,000-foot peak in Peru, where our party tried a route earlier attempted by Lionel Terray; the other was an attempt on the South Face of Mt. Logan. I have climbed numerous summits in the Canadian Rockies and am also active in cross-country skiing and ski mountaineering.

As a boy I learned to make jerky from an elderly Indian lady in central British Columbia. Jerky keeps for months or years (if not eaten first). It beats the cost of freeze-dried meat and (if made properly) tastes a lot better. It can be eaten as is or added to any boiled dish. In camp, you can make it from moose, deer, or caribou (or at home, from beef).

Slice lean meat (with the grain) into ¾-inch strips. Fill a large pot with boiling water and add enough salt to float an egg (it takes about 6 tablespoons — ⅜ cup — of salt to 4 cups of water; so be sure you have plenty of salt on hand). Tie a cord around the meat, and dip the bundle into the brine (or just dump the strips in loose, and ladle them out later). Boil meat in brine for 10 minutes. Jerk the meat out, and hang it to drip. Lay the strips of meat on a screen over a campfire, and smoke until a thin skin forms on the outside. Put the dried, smoked meat in a cloth flour sack, and hang up in a cool dry place. (If the jerky is made at home, dry the meat on a cookie sheet in a warm oven for several hours.) ❞

William Lokey
MOUNTAIN McMUFFINS

2-ounce can freeze-dried ham
Freeze-dried eggs equal to 2 servings
2 ounces margarine (or to taste)
2 English muffins (or substitute, to
taste)

4 ounces cheese
Package hollandaise sauce mix
Salt and pepper

Reconstitute ham as directed on container. Add ham to reconstituted eggs. Melt a little margarine in frying pan over low heat. Add ham-egg mixture. Cook and stir gently till eggs are no longer runny. Prepare hollandaise sauce according to package directions. Toast muffins over stove, and spread with margarine. Put muffins in heated cups or other suitable containers. Pile a good helping of eggs and ham on top of muffins, add thick slices of cheese, and pour hollandaise sauce over the whole thing. Season with salt and pepper to taste. Serves 2.

William (Bill) Lokey of Tacoma, Washington has climbed extensively in the Pacific Northwest, Alaska, Mexico, France, Africa, and New Zealand. He works for the Department of Emergency Services, in the State Disaster Preparedness Planning Office. In past years Bill has had extensive experience in the Arctic and Antarctic. While he was working for the United States Antarctic Research Program, his activities included three winters in the Antarctic at various stations. In 1974 he made a round-the-world snowshoe trek. This unlikely sounding feat was accomplished by his snowshoeing in a small circle around the geographic South Pole at a latitude of approximately 89° 59' 59"! He spent six summers on the Juneau Icefield, a vast expanse of ice and rock in southeast Alaska. He climbed new routes on Alaska's Mt. Hubbard and Mt. Vancouver and in April 1980, climbed Mt. McKinley via the Pioneer Ridge.

❝ Sometimes life on the icefield was a dog's life. One late May I was leader of a small group that snowshoed in the ten miles of trail and glacier from Juneau to the Arctic Sciences Institute's main camp at about 3500 feet. We dug the snow away from the door, started our weather observations, and launched the annual spring housecleaning and fix-up that preceded the arrival of students and staff.

A big box of unlabeled cans that had collected over the years had been stashed away the previous fall. As this camp is stocked by helicopter and the cost of supplies is high, nothing is wasted; so I made it a camp rule that we had to eat four of the unlabeled cans a day till all were gone. Some contained fruit—good; most weren't bad; but the hash (beef or corned beef) seemed to be low quality and hadn't been improved by a winter of freezing and thawing. But we ate it. A few weeks later, a staff member showed up inquiring about the eight cans of dog food he had left in the storage box the year before. It seemed that his constant companion, a husky, was hungry. ❞

Gary Lyon
IGLOO CREEK FRENCH TOAST

4 slices of bread
Freeze-dried or dried scrambled egg
    mix equal to 2-person serving
Dry milk, about half the amount of
    dried egg mix
Warm water

Butter (optional)
Bacon bar (optional)
Syrup (powdered or freeze-dried mix;
    or boil brown sugar and a little
    water together)

At home, cut bread slices into 1-inch squares, and set them out until they are stale. Seal bread in plastic bag to carry. At camp, mix dried eggs and dry milk together in a plastic bag, and add enough warm water to make a slightly thick liquid. Dunk bread pieces into egg-milk mixture, and brown in frying pan (a nonstick coated pan works well; or fry in a little butter). Sprinkle browned bread squares with crumbled bacon bar, add butter if you have it, and serve with warm syrup. This makes a good 1-pan meal served with a hot drink such as coffee, cocoa, or orange flavor instant drink. Serves 2.

Gary Lyon is a wildlife artist who lives in Anchorage, Alaska.

❝ I came to Alaska in the early 1970's to find wilderness, wild animals, and few cities. Alaska has all that I looked for. I make my living by painting in watercolors and other media. My favorite subject matter is animals in their natural wild setting.

For me, backpacking is probably the most rewarding way of experiencing the wilderness. I have hiked on the Kenai Peninsula, in the Wrangell Mountains northeast of Anchorage, in the Chugach Mountains in southern Alaska east of Anchorage, in Mount McKinley (now Denali) National Park, and in other remote areas. The national park is the best place to see wildlife: ptarmigan, golden eagles, caribou, moose—and grizzly bears, which cannot be seen in many other places.

Once while backpacking above timberline (grassline?) in the Chugach Mountains, my companion and I were returning to camp after a grueling all-day trek. The wind was so strong that we had to lie down and wait for a lull, then run for twenty to fifty yards till the wind picked up. When we got to camp—the camp was gone! All that remained was our stove and the front tent peg with its line blowing in the wind. We set out down a creek bed for lower ground and picked up some of our belongings as we went. Wet sleeping bags had been blown a mile. Many things were never found. Of our food, only cheese, sausage, and a few crackers survived. Freeze-dried food sacks were torn, the contents soaked and useless. We learned that in backpacking the unexpected always happens. One should carry some durable food for that inevitable adventure. ❞

Leah Niemoth
EGG TORTILLA

Oil
2 tortillas
2 fresh eggs
Seasonings to taste

Prepare each Egg Tortilla separately unless pan is large. Put oil in frying pan, and fry tortilla till soft. Gently crack the eggshell, and carefully let the egg slip out on top of the tortilla. Put lid over pan, and cook tortilla and egg till just done. Eat immediately. Serves 2.

Leah Niemoth, a self-taught wildlife watercolorist and naturalist, now lives in Kailua Kona, Hawaii, after spending twenty-five years in Alaska.

❝ In Alaska I frequently ran into dangerous big game animals such as moose and bear, but was never harmed by them as I have a deep respect for their territory. As to the smaller animals, I always shared a little of my food with them by such methods as leaving a bit of peanut butter on a stick. My favorite hike was in the Chugach Mountains in search of the illusive morel (an edible fungus) and the early spring wild flowers that grew along with it. When I had some of the fresh-picked Alaskan morels (*Morchella augusticips*) that grow on the mountainsides along Turnagin Arm, I prepared them in this way. I brushed or blew the dirt from them, sliced them in half lengthwise, and cooked them in butter in a small frying pan until tender—it takes just a few minutes. Then I poured in a little dry sherry. Everyone dipped in with quarter-slices of a good whole wheat bread.

My favorite Hawaiian hike is up 8271-foot Mt. Hualalai, a dormant volcano on the west side of Hawaii, the largest and southeasternmost of the Hawaiian Islands. Hiking up old lava flows, I often slip in holes that formed after the lava cooled. My shoes wear out in just a few such hikes. There is no natural water on this peak—in a pinch, I get moisture from berries, just as the endangered nene goose does. Breakfast is always eaten accompanied by the singing of the rare honeycreeper birds I am studying on Hualalai. ❞

Bob Swenson
SOURDOUGH HOTCAKES

1 cup sourdough starter*
2½ cups flour
2 cups warm water
1 egg (or equivalent in reconstituted
    dried egg)
¼ cup dry milk
2 tablespoons oil or melted bacon grease
1 cup mountain blueberries or
    presoaked dry applesauce
    (optional)

2 tablespoons sugar
1 teaspoon salt
1 teaspoon baking soda
Fat for frying
Syrup (of berries or applesauce)

Well before trip, obtain sourdough starter. On the trip, after deciding there will be time next morning for sourdough pancakes, mix up the starter with the flour and warm water. This batter should be placed overnight in a covered pot, in a warm protected part of the tent. Next morning, first of all, put 1 cup of this batter in your starter jar, if you want some for next time. To the remaining batter add egg, milk, oil or melted grease, fruit (if any), sugar, salt, and baking soda. Fry hotcakes in fat or oil, and serve with syrup. The Ultimate Syrup is made by cooking a copious amount of blueberries or huckleberries with sugar the night before, and reheating in the morning. You can also use a dried apple-sugar-cinnamon syrup or other flavor. Serves 2 or 3.*

Bob Swenson of Bellevue, Washington started climbing in the mid-1950's when he lived in Yakima. He has made numerous ascents in the Cascades and Olympics, has climbed in the Tetons of Wyoming and the Sawtooths of Idaho, and is active in mountain rescue work.

❞❞ Sourdough hotcakes are a delight in the mountains, but require special effort. Transport the cup of starter in a pint-sized jar with a tight lid, well sealed in a double plastic sack. Otherwise, it may expand and seek every corner of your pack till you have to wring it out of your socks to have enough for the morrow. You must also nurture the batter carefully overnight, being sure to issue an 'under pain of death' warning to those who might make late night visits and kick the pot. ❞❞

---

*Starter is basically a combination of milk and flour kept warm till a special bacterial action occurs. It can be made by keeping a cup of raw milk warm for 24 hours, stirring in a cup of flour, and letting the mixture stand in an uncovered crock or glass jar at about 80° for 2 to 5 days, till it turns sour and bubbly. However, this doesn't always work. It is more reliable to buy starter mix at a specialty food shop. And the best way, if it can be done, is to get starter from a friend. At home, between uses, refrigerate or freeze the stuff.

"Timmy has certainly been nice and quiet the last hour."

Allen Steck
SCHMARREN PANCAKES

1 cup flour
1 cup liquid milk
2 eggs (fresh or equivalent dried)
¼ cup sugar

1 tablespoon salt
Butter
Berries if available

Mix together all ingredients except butter and berries. A tablespoon of salt sounds like a lot, but a salty-sweet taste is sought. When the frying pan is hot, put in a lump of butter to melt. Pour in enough batter to make the desired size of pancake. With a spatula, turn cake when bottom is browned. Fried plain in butter, these are called Palashinken *("pancakes" in Austrian dialect). However, after they are fried on one side, they are often cut into small pieces and totally cooked to a golden brown. Then they are called* Schmarren *and are usually served with a very tart fresh fruit, such as blueberries or blackberries. Austrians use* Preisselbeeren, *European berries related to huckleberries. This recipe serves 2 to 4.*

Allen (Al) Steck of Berkeley, California is a writer, photographer, trekking consultant, and longtime climber. In the late 1940's and early 1950's he made many difficult rock ascents in Yosemite, and in the Dolomites and elsewhere in the Alps. In the 1950's and 1960's he made the first ascent of the North Face of Mt. Waddington, the highest peak in British Columbia; was on the first ascent of the East Peak of Huandoy in Peru; climbed Mt. Logan by the Hummingbird Ridge, a new route; and was on various Himalayan expeditions. His climbs in the 1970's included Mt. Kenya in Africa, Pik Lenin in the Pamirs of Russia, and peaks in the Himalaya, the Hindu Kush, and the Andes. Al's latest major expedition was a first ascent of Paiju Peak in Pakistan with the Pakistan Alpine Club.

Al is founder and an editor of *Ascent*, Sierra Club mountaineering journal. In 1980 *Ascent* was converted to a soft-cover book edited by Al Steck and Steve Roper. The pair also coauthored *Fifty Classic Climbs of North America*. Al was the first recipient (with Norman Clyde) of the Sierra Club's Francis P. Farquhar Mountaineering Award.

❝ My climbing efforts have not been without comic relief. In the 1950's, the late Willi Unsoeld and I made an attempt on the East Buttress of El Capitan in Yosemite. We were retreating at dusk and chose a direct way down the cliff—not the route of ascent. One of the rappels landed us in a bay tree that grew horizontally out of the sheer cliff, with no ledge. The thing was 'in heat'—with lots of pollen. I was overcome with sneezing during our entire time in that tree. Have you ever tried to rappel entirely from a tree, and in the dark? I finally set the rappel, only to discover when I put my weight on the rope that I had placed the rope over Willi's leg as well as around the tree trunk. There was much laughter and pain that night. ❞

Betty J. Tucker-Bryan
NOMAD CAKES

½ cup peanuts
¼ cup soy granules
¼ cup sunflower seeds
¼ cup roasted sesame seeds
1 envelope fresh egg substitute or dried
    egg mix
1 teaspoon dry onion flakes

1 teaspoon dried vegetable flakes
Dried dill weed to taste
¼ teaspoon salt
¼ teaspoon garlic powder
Butter, oil, or margarine
Sour cream sauce mix (optional)

At home, pulverize nuts, soy granules, and seeds in blender. Mix in the egg, onion and vegetable flakes, and seasonings. Put mixture in a double plastic bag for transport. In camp, stir just enough water into the dry ingredients so you can form the mixture into small patties. Fry slowly in butter, oil, or margarine until cakes are lightly browned on both sides. Sour cream sauce mix, reconstituted according to package directions, is great on top of patties.

Betty J. Tucker-Bryan of Yellowstone National Park was the first woman to make a solo hike of the 140-mile length of Death Valley in California. The trailless hike, in March 1972, was carefully planned, with rendezvous points for food and water arranged with her husband, Scott. This experience led Betty to form the Death Valley Hiker's Association. She also became involved in plans for the proposed 2500-mile Desert Trail, which will stretch from Canada to Mexico, going through parts of Idaho, Oregon, Nevada, and California. It will be a point-to-point route, probably with a wide corridor along which hikers can travel with compass and topographical maps. Betty is coordinator for the 550-mile portion in California, part of which will pass through Death Valley along the general route of her 1972 hike. She is also involved, with her husband, in geyser research, work which will take them backpacking to over twenty-five foreign countries.

❝ Long desert hikes require careful planning. For one such undertaking, I put out caches of food and water a month or so ahead of time. I thought the food was well planned to last and to taste good. In one cache, I placed travel cakes of rolled oats, sesame seeds, and alfalfa seeds. Sharing the coffee-can cache was a tightly sealed water bottle. By the time I could reach the cache, strange things had happened. Digging the can out of the sand, I was greeted by a horrible smell of mold. Inside the can, the travel cakes had turned lime green. The water bottle had developed a drip; the drip, tiny but enduring, had sprouted the alfalfa seeds. I harvested the crop of sprouts and enjoyed an unexpected green salad. ❞

One-Burner Baking

"But his biscuits are sensational!"

Bradford Angier
BANNOCK

1 cup all-purpose flour
1 teaspoon double action baking powder
¼ teaspoon salt
3 tablespoons margarine

2 tablespoons dry milk
Water, as necessary for desired
consistency of dough

At home, sift flour before measuring. Then sift together flour, baking powder, and salt. Cut margarine into dry ingredients until the mixture resembles coarse meal — use two dull knives, an electric mixer at low speed, or a pastry blender. Add dry milk. Carry mix in a plastic bag. In camp, stir mix lightly, and add enough water to make a moderately soft dough that can be cooked as bread or biscuits in a covered greased frying pan over low to moderate heat. Turn as necessary for even baking. Serves 1 to 2.

Bradford Angier, one of America's leading exponents of backpacking and other outdoor pursuits, lives in Hudson Hope, British Columbia. He was formerly a magazine and advertising executive, but he and his wife, Vena, left early careers to establish a home in the woods on the Peace River in western Canada. Bradford learned basic wilderness skills and woodcraft from trappers, hunters, prospectors, and traders of the region. By experience and experiment, he expanded his new-found knowledge. Since then he has written more than thirty books, among them *Wilderness Cookery, Home in Your Pack, The Field Guide to Edible Wild Plants,* and *Living Off the Country.*

❝ This bannock mix can be made up ahead of time in any quantity — it will stay fresh for six weeks or more on the trail if kept sealed, dry, and reasonably cool. It has multiple short-notice uses — for oven drop biscuits, baked fruit cobblers, shortcakes, flapjacks, dumplings, etc.

Where a campfire is possible, you can make a handy hot bread that requires no utensils. Cut and preheat a green hardwood stick, the diameter of a rake handle, so trimmed that several projecting stubs will keep the dough in place. Birch is a particularly sweet wood for this purpose. When the fire is going, add just enough water to the mix to make a firm dough. Shape dough into a long thin roll an inch or less thick. Wind the dough ribbon around the preheated stick. Hold the bannock in the heat, occasionally turning it, for a couple of minutes. When the crust has formed, lean the stick between the fringes of the fire and a reflecting surface such as a log or rock for 15 minutes or so, to form a tasty brown spiral. Or just shove the sharpened end of the stick into the ground beside the fire, and turn it now and then while readying the rest of the meal. ❞

Dave DeJong
QUICKIE CORNBREAD

1 cup yellow cornmeal
1 cup biscuit mix
2 tablespoons dried egg
½ teaspoon salt

2 tablespoons cooking oil
1 cup water
Grease for frying pan
Brown sugar

At home, mix the cornmeal, biscuit mix, egg, and salt together. Pack in plastic bag. In camp, add oil and water, and mix. Pour the batter into a well-greased frying pan (preferably one with a nonstick coating). Cover and cook over low heat. After 5 to 7 minutes, sprinkle brown sugar on top of bread, and carefully turn it over. Cook for another 5 to 7 minutes (or longer, if it appears to need more baking time). When baking over a one-burner stove, the heat from the stove can be spread more evenly if you place a metal jar lid under the frying pan. Without it, the loaf may very well burn black in the center. Serves 2 to 4.

Dave DeJong of Wenatchee, Washington has enjoyed many family backpacking trips on the Wonderland Trail in Mount Rainier National Park.

❝ You expect a lot of food to disappear when backpacking with a crew of two adults and five kids, of whom several are strapping teenagers with huge appetites. In addition to the usual assortment of freeze-dried and dehydrated foods, our supplies usually included several homemade mixes for various breads. We discovered that with a little patience, it is possible to bake some quite palatable breads on top of a one-burner camp stove. The kids moved in hungrily whenever they caught the aroma of fresh bread.

Besides the cornbread, a bannock bread can be made from the following mix assembled at home: 2 cups white flour, 2 tablespoons dry milk, 2 tablespoons dry egg, 2 teaspoons baking powder, and ½ teaspoon salt. In camp, when you are ready for fresh mountain-man bread, add 2 tablespoons cooking oil, ½ cup raisins (optional), and enough water to stiffen and mix the dough. Bake as for Quickie Cornbread, in a covered greased nonstick frying pan, over low heat, with a metal jar lid under the pan. Turn very cautiously after 5 to 7 minutes, bake till done, and serve hot from the pan with melted butter, jam, or honey. ❞

Michael Frome
DISHWASHER'S DELIGHT

¼ cup (⅛ pound) butter	1 cup biscuit mix (or more)
Dried eggs for 2 servings	⅓ cup water per cup biscuit mix
Prefried bacon to taste	Salt and pepper

Melt butter in 1-quart mess kit or frying pan, over low heat (don't skimp on butter). Reconstitute eggs as directed on package, put into the melted butter in pan, and crumble in the prefried bacon. While eggs cook slowly, stir up the biscuit mix and water to make a large ½-inch-thick biscuit to fit on top of the eggs (if necessary vary the amount or shape to fit the pan). Cover pan, and cook slowly till biscuit is done. Add salt and pepper to taste. Serves 2. This makes a breakfast (or other meal) that provides lots of energy, with protein, starch, and fats. It is especially good in cold weather. (At home, remove the biscuit mix from its box, and pack the needed amount in a plastic bag for transport.)

Michael Frome of Alexandria, Virginia has been an exponent of wilderness for many years. On foot, canoe, and horseback he has explored wild lands throughout the United States and abroad. His outdoor articles have appeared in leading magazines and newspapers. His books include *Whose Woods These Are, Strangers in High Places*, and *Battle for the Wilderness*. He was visiting professor of environmental studies at the University of Vermont in 1978.

❝ The point that strikes me most on reflection about outdoor cooking is the way so many delights in rustling up a meal around the campfire seem to have been banished to oblivion by the wide variety of freeze-dried and dehydrated foods. Now the secret is to add a few individual touches to those packaged items that weigh so little and provide such varied menus. Of course, the campfire itself is largely gone, now that open fires are banned in so many areas. One must know not how to start a fire with wet tinder, but how to work pressure stoves.

Horace Kephart, the old master of camping and woodcraft whose book *Camp Cookery* was published in 1934, knew nothing of instant fires and powdered dinners. 'First and above all, be plain in the woods,' he instructed. 'We seek the woods to escape civilization for a time, and all that suggests it. Let us sometimes broil our venison on a sharpened stick and serve it on a sheet of bark. It gets us closer to Nature, and closer to those good old times. It is one of the blessings of wilderness life that it shows us how few things we need in order to be perfectly happy.' ❞

Peter Simer
CORNMEAL FLAT BREAD

½ cup flour
½ cup cornmeal
½ cup water
Pinch salt

Margarine
Cheese, thinly sliced
Bacon bits, or sliced sausage

Mix flour, cornmeal, and water. Form into flat patties. Fry in frying pan lightly greased with margarine. When bottoms of patties are golden brown, turn them over. Place cheese and meat on top of patties, cover frying pan, and continue to cook until bottoms are nicely browned and the cheese is melted. (If cooking can be done over a campfire, fry patties till brown on both sides; place cheese and meat on top; melt cheese by placing hot coals on the frying pan lid for 5 to 10 minutes.) Serves 1 or 2.

Peter Simer is the director of the National Outdoor Leadership School of Lander, Wyoming. His students and staff adapted the cornmeal and Syrian bread recipes for backpacking. Peter's extensive outdoor experience includes long periods in the Rockies and Cascades, as well as considerable time in Alaska, Baja California, Kenya, and the French Alps. He started instructing in NOLS in 1970.

❝ This nonprofit organization was founded in 1965 to train interested persons in the skills and judgment necessary for leadership in outdoor activities. The courses emphasize both the enjoyment and the conservation of the wild outdoors. With courses lasting from 14 to 114 days, there is a demand for good food made from grocery store ingredients.

Another good recipe for outdoor baking—when you have time for it—is Syrian Bread. This version was created on Mt. McKinley to supplement the repetitious diet of a six-week expedition. You need three ¼-ounce envelopes of dry yeast, ¼ cup warm water, a little sugar, and 1 cup each white and whole wheat flour (plus some extra flour). To water that is warm to the touch (not hot), add sugar and yeast. Let it work 5 to 10 minutes. Stir in flour. Knead, adding more flour as necessary, until the ball of dough is smooth. Put dough in billycan and cover with damp cloth. Let rise about an hour in a warm place. Punch down the dough. Pinch off lumps an inch in diameter. Flatten the lumps between palms of hands, and let rise 15 minutes. Place lumps of dough one by one on a pan lid, or other flat surface, covered with a floured plastic sack. Using a clean water bottle for a rolling pin, roll each lump out to ⅛-inch thickness. Cook each piece separately in a covered frying pan, with no grease. When loaf puffs up in the middle, flip it over and cook on the other side till golden brown. Slice finished loaf in half—there should be a pocket in each half. Serve with butter, or with a spicy lentil filling. **❞**

*"**Survival training**? I thought I signed up for Chef Rudolfo's Gourmet Tour of the Catskills!"*

Bill Kemsley
HORN CREEK BANNOCKS

2 cups biscuit mix
⅔ cup water (approximate)
Margarine for frying pan
Jam, etc., to taste

Combine biscuit mix and enough water to make a stiff dough. Pat a chunk of the dough into an inch-thick cake, as large as can fit into your frying pan, and fry it very slowly in margarine, while turning often. It takes a long time, but it is a great dish if you have the time and a lot to talk about. Serves 2 to 4.

Bill Kemsley, founder and former editor of *Backpacker* magazine, was born and raised in Michigan and now lives in Greenwich, Connecticut.

❝ I used to sail and in the mid-1950's was a mountain climber. I practiced in the Shawangunks in southeastern New York, where I put up a couple of new routes. I also climbed in other eastern rock climbing areas. I have made ascents in the Bugaboos of British Columbia, and in the Cascades, Tetons, and Rockies. In fact I believe I have been on mountaineering or backpacking trips in every major mountain range in the continental United States. My wife, Marcella, and our six children now find that backpacking is a great family activity.

We have backpacked in Great Britain, the Virgin Islands, some of the choicest hiking areas of the U.S., and several provinces in Canada. The area we like best is the Catskill Mountains in southeastern New York west of the Hudson River. The Catskills are only a two-hour drive from our home.

An exciting family trip in recent years was a seven-day backpack into the Grand Canyon. At that time our oldest child was thirteen, our youngest (carried by my wife) was nine months, and we had three toddlers. I don't believe in trying to get children to set records in hiking; but we couldn't help being proud of our youngsters, who hiked eleven miles in one day and made a vertical elevation gain of 4000 feet in about four and a half hours. On that trip, we spent an entire afternoon cooking and eating bannocks with strawberry jam and Danish salami. We used up an entire box of biscuit mix and had an enormously good time. ❞

John Rugge
ADIRONDACK SWEET ROLLS

2 cups biscuit mix
½ cup sugar
⅔ cup water (approximate)
1 teaspoon cinnamon
4 to 6 tablespoons margarine
    (approximate)

½ cup raisins —or better yet, fresh
    berries in season (blueberries,
    wild strawberries, raspberries,
    etc.)
½ cup powdered (icing) sugar
Boiling water (a little)

Combine biscuit mix with ¼ cup of the sugar. Add water to make a firm dough. Pat out an inch or less thick. Cover dough with remaining ¼ cup sugar, cinnamon, a couple of tablespoons melted margarine, and fruit. Cut dough into strips, and roll into cylinders (or roll up the whole slab, and slice into cylinders ¾ to 1 inch thick). Melt some of the margarine in frying pan, carefully lay the rounds of sweet rolls in the pan, cover, and cook over low heat. Meanwhile mix the powdered sugar with 2 tablespoons melted margarine, add boiling water a few drops at a time, and stir until icing reaches desired creamy consistency. Spread or drizzle it over the rolls when they are ready to serve. Serves 2 to 4.

John Rugge, M.D. lives in Chestertown in northeastern New York State. He is a canoeist, and with James West Davidson is coauthor of *The Complete Wilderness Paddler*. The book is a guide to canoeing and expedition technique, and it tells the story of a trip down the Moisie River in Labrador and Quebec. The two men also produced a motion picture of another canoe expedition that started in the barren highlands of Labrador.

❝ My first long canoe trip was when I was eleven—a ten-day excursion through the Adirondacks, on which my father came up with blueberry sweet rolls. I don't remember the rolls very well, but I do remember the Boy Scouts who camped near us that morning. They each had a bowl of crushed cornflakes for breakfast. My father invited a couple of them over to share our bounty. When they returned to their own camp, we overheard one of them tell the others, 'Hey, that kid over there, he's got his own guide!'
    Another treat in the wilderness that no one seems to think of is popcorn. The cooking technique is about the same as at home, but use a frying pan with a cover; this avoids the nuisance of burning your cooking pot. Preheat margarine in the frying pan over medium-hot heat. Put in a couple of test kernels to help avoid scorching the corn. When it is popped, add salt to taste. Lean back against a tree—and if the night is right, catch the aurora borealis late show. ❞

Gerry Wolfram
BISCUIT-CAKE DESSERT

1 ⅛ cups all-purpose flour
2 teaspoons baking powder
⅓ teaspoon cream of tartar
½ teaspon salt
¼ cup dry milk

¼ cup shortening (any type not
    needing refrigeration)
Water, about ⅓ cup
Chopped dried fruit, wild berries, or
    nuts, to taste

At home, sift dry ingredients together, and work in the shortening to consistency of coarse meal. Transport mix in plastic bag. In camp, add enough water for a soft dough, about ⅓ cup. Add fruits or nuts in desired quantity. Grease frying pan well, and pour in the dough. To bake, cover pan, and brown cake on one side over low heat. Flip over, and continue to bake till done. If you can have a campfire, cook the first side in covered frying pan. Turn cake, bank coals, and prop up the pan so the heat reflects on the cake to finish cooking it. Serves 2.

Sufficient basic biscuit mix to provide cake, biscuits, and pancakes for 2 people for 2 weeks can be made by using 9 cups flour, ⅓ cup baking powder, 2 ½ teaspoons cream of tartar, 4 teaspoons salt, 2 cups dry milk, and 2 cups shortening. In camp, add water to part of mix, in proportion needed for biscuit dough, pancake batter, etc.

Gerry Wolfram and his wife, Gwyn, live in St. Catherines, Ontario, not far from Niagara Falls. Gerry is an outdoor writer; host of a TV show on weekend fishing; wildlife photographer; and participant in such outdoor activities as snowshoeing, backpacking, white-water canoeing, and big game hunting with bow and arrow. He is the author of *Walk into Winter: A Complete Snowshoeing & Winter Camping Guide.*

❞❞ Outdoor meals are often memorable largely because of circumstances; spend enough hours out in a blizzard, and anything hot—even scorched wieners and beans—assumes a gourmet rating. But a meal becomes great only with a side dish such as a panful of butter-melting, finger-scorching biscuits such as my wife, Gwyn, whips up, seemingly in seconds under any conditions. A cross-country ski or snowshoe luncheon takes on added prestige if accompanied by spiced red wine heated on a one-burner stove. I never go on a long canoe trip without taking a head or two of cabbage along. Cabbage keeps well, provides vitamins, and dresses up almost any kind of meal, from a cabbage-peanut butter sandwich to a cabbage-wild blueberry salad served with smoked trout and all the trimmings. ❞❞

Beverages, Salads, and Snacks

Jene Crenshaw and H.V.J. Kilness
DATE MILK SHAKE

⅓ *cup (5 tablespoons) dry milk*
Date powder, to taste
¾ *cup cold water*

Combine dry milk and date powder in cup. Fill cup with cold water and stir, for a delicious date-flavored milk shake. Serves 1.

Jene Crenshaw and Helen (H.V.J.) Kilness live at Big Bear Lake at 7000 feet elevation in the San Bernardino Mountains of Southern California. Jene and Helen are copublishers and editors of *Summit*, the oldest general-circulation mountaineering magazine in the United States. *Summit* began in 1955, unique in its field—even today there are few similar national publications. In the years since its inception, *Summit* has grown and expanded. One of its outstanding features in recent years is its fine color reproductions of mountain scenes. In 1978 the American Alpine Club awarded a special citation to Helen and Jene for their service to mountaineering through the publication.

❦❦ We saw the need for such a periodical—so we got together and started *Summit*. At first the magazine catered primarily to skiers. But we soon found out that climbers and hikers are much more avid readers. When *Summit* began, there was no other publication like it in the United States except for the various mountaineering club journals, which serve a different need.

We are both mountaineers of long standing. We have climbed most major peaks in the Sierra Nevada, as well as having made ascents in Colorado, Washington, and Alaska. We have also been to the top of Picacho del Diablo (the climber's name for Cerro de la Encantado), a remote 10,125-foot peak in Baja, California. We have not been on any long expeditions, mainly because we cannot be away for more than ten days at a time.

For our climbing and hiking outings, we like cooked cereal for breakfast, with raisins, dates, or nuts, and dry milk added. Our trail lunches are often whole wheat snack crackers with cheese and a gorp bag filled with assorted nuts, raisins, dried banana chips, etc. We do like a date milk shake to go with it, and in our area we have had no difficulty finding packaged date powder in various stores. ❦❦

William N. Prater
SHERPA GROG

2 parts hot cocoa mix
2 parts dry milk
1 part sugar
Miniature marshmallows (optional)

At home, combine cocoa mix, dry milk, and sugar; add marshmallows if desired. Transport mix in plastic bag. In camp, measure about ⅓ cup of mix into cup, and fill cup to brim with boiling water. Stir.

William (Bill) Prater, who lives in Wenatchee, in central Washington, has been an active mountaineer since 1949. He has made numerous climbs in the Cascades, including the first winter ascent of Mt. Stuart. He has also climbed in the Rockies and in the Presidential Range of New Hampshire; in 1965 was on the first ascent of 13,905-foot Mt. Kennedy in the St. Elias Range in Yukon Territory; and in 1976 climbed 20,320-foot Mt. McKinley.

Bill was the first commercial manufacturer of lightweight snowshoes especially designed for mountain use. He had had much personal experience in floundering around on Pacific Northwest peaks on heavy unwieldy wooden snowshoes with poor bindings. Thus inspired, he began to manufacture radically different snowshoes that included lightweight metal frames, traction devices, and a new type of binding that would accommodate any boot. His snowshoes caused a revolution in winter climbing in the areas for which they had been adapted and also proved practical for widespread recreational use.

❝ We began our own snowshoe manufacturing firm in 1971. At first we made bindings, traction kits, and ice axe baskets. In 1973 we started making aluminum-frame snowshoes in three models, and we added more models later. Our snowshoes were soon in use on major mountain expeditions from McKinley to the Antarctic, on K2, and to over 21,500 feet on Everest. We sold the controlling interest in our company in 1977, but I am still a consultant to the firm, designing and testing snowshoes and other new products which may be marketable in the future.

I devised Sherpa Grog on winter snowshoe outings in the Stuart Range of the Cascades. It works well as part of an eating 'system' that requires only a way to heat water, and a cup and spoon. At breakfast, mix the cereal in a cup, follow it with cocoa, and swab out the cup with snow. For dinner, start with soup in the cup; follow this with a mixture of instant potato, cheese, corned beef, lots of butter, and seasonings; end up with a cup of Sherpa Grog. Again clean out the cup with snow or water, and it's ready for the next meal. It's a good way to cut down on camp chores. ❞

Bradford B. Van Diver
RUSSIAN TEA MIX

2 cups orange flavor instant drink
4 scoops unsweetened lemonade-flavor
   mix
¾ cup unsweetened instant tea (plain
   or with lemon)

1 cup sugar
2 teaspoons cinnamon
1 teaspoon allspice
1 teaspoon ground cloves
Hot water

At home, combine dry ingredients. Pack in plastic bags for carrying. In camp, stir 2 teaspoons of tea mix into a cup of hot water.

Bradford (Brad) Van Diver is a professor in the Department of Geological Sciences at the State University, College of Arts and Sciences, at Potsdam, New York. He is a longtime climber, and author of *Rocks and Routes of the North Country, New York* and *Upstate New York Geology Field Guide*.

❝ I began climbing in the Boulder, Colorado area in 1946 and made many rock climbs there, and later on 14,255-foot Longs Peak in Rocky Mountain National Park. Bill Eubank and I are responsible for several first ascents in both areas. I have made many ascents in the North Cascades and traveled and climbed in the Canadian Rockies. I have climbed Mexico's three highest volcanic peaks, Popocatepetl, 17,887 feet (twice); Ixtaccihuatl, 17,343 feet; and Orizaba (Citlaltepetl), 18,701 feet. I spent two years in Bolivia as an exploration geologist and made some minor climbs in the foothills of the Andes. In the 1970's, I made numerous ascents in the Zillertal Alps of Austria and climbed Mt. Blanc and the Matterhorn. Since coming to New York in 1965, I have climbed extensively in the Adirondacks. I have long been a downhill skier and am now into cross-country skiing and white-water kayaking.

A cup of Russian Tea should help get you to your summit. A couple of other camp beverages are good and easy to make. Stir 3 or 4 teaspoons of fruit-flavored gelatin dessert into a cup of hot water (add orange flavor instant drink or sweetened lemonade mix to taste); or put equal parts of hot cocoa mix and instant coffee—each in normal amounts—into a cup of hot water. ❞

Richard and Joyce Murlless
SWAMP SALAD

1 small cabbage head
1 can crushed pineapple, 8¼- or 13¼-ounce size
1 cup nuts (soy nuts, pecans, blanched almonds, or any favorite)
Mayonnaise

Dice cabbage. Drain all juice from pineapple. Combine all ingredients. Soy nuts are dried and roasted soybeans, and can be found salted or unsalted. Unsalted seem best for this salad. (Mayonnaise may spoil after a few days of hot weather, once the jar has been opened.)

Joyce and Richard Murlless of Savannah, Georgia operate a nonprofit educational corporation that offers trips organized for two types of groups. Some are for anybody who wants to sign on; some are for organizations such as schools, churches, nature centers, and clubs. Richard is coauthor with Constance Stallings of *Hiker's Guide to the Smokies*.

❝ We are always learning about the environment wherever we go. We take groups snorkeling to study coral reefs. We have been involved in a research project to study loggerheads—300-pound sea turtles that lay their eggs on the beaches. We also offer instruction in subjects such as edible plants, botany, camping skills, and ecology.

Our trips cover a variety of activities and environments. Some feature canoeing, with one day to five days of paddling on our lazy southern rivers. On others we set up a beach base camp for backpackers in the recently established Cumberland Island National Seashore off the southern tip of Georgia. This island has salt marshes, high dunes, maritime forests of live oaks, long tidal beaches of hard-packed fine white sand, and immensely varied wildlife.

We also visit swamps, such as the Everglades and the 40-mile-long Okefenokee Swamp in southeastern Georgia and northeastern Florida. Everyone wants to see alligators, but the creatures are sometimes elusive in cold weather. Usually we see many of them. We have taken trips to Garden Key, one of the Dry Tortugas, small sand and coral islands west of Key West. We have made trips to Guatemala, staying in native hotels or camping out while studying the wildlife of rain forests, volcanoes, and deserts. Guatemalan backpacks are interspersed with trips in native dugout canoes.

In studying recipe books put out by mountain clubs, we have noticed that in the western United States, outdoor people apparently eat much larger quantities than we do here in the South. I don't know why we can manage with smaller servings. It may be due to our low elevation, or to the warmer climate. ❞

Evelyn-Mae Nikolaus
MOUNTAIN SALAD

3-ounce package gelatin dessert (lime or other fruit flavor)
Dried vegetable flakes, 3-ounce can, about
2 cups (16 ounces) boiling water

At home divide dry gelatin dessert into 2 quart-sized "boilable" plastic bags* or quart resealable plastic bags. Divide vegetable flakes into 2 small sandwich bags or squares of plastic wrap. Twist to seal these and insert into bags with gelatin, then seal the larger bags well. These will each make 2 servings. Mark bags with appropriate amount of water to use. In camp, several hours before mealtime if possible, or as the first step in meal preparation, put vegetable flakes into water, 1 cup for 2 servings; bring water to boil, allowing vegetables to rehydrate. When the water is boiling, add to gelatin in bag, and stir to dissolve if necessary. Fold bag over or reseal if possible. Put in a cool place such as snowbank or shallow ice-cold mountain stream (secure bags with rocks or cord so they won't float away). Very cold moving water will set the gelatin while the rest of the meal is cooking.

Evelyn-Mae Nikolaus lives in Independence, California in the high desert east of the Sierra Nevada. She and her husband have been hiking in remote corners of the Southwest for over twenty years and have also sampled canoeing in Minnesota's lake country.

❞❞ I have hiked through some thirty-five 10,000-foot mountain passes in the Sierra Nevada, and also in Zion, Brice, and Grand Canyon national parks and elsewhere. For our backpacking trips I make food lists for each meal and pack the food carefully. I have found 'boilable' plastic bags* useful in countless ways. We carry nearly every food item in these bags. Perishable items such as bacon can be kept cool for some time by sealing them in 'boilable' bags and wrapping them inside sleeping bags, which provide dandy insulation. I can heat-seal individual servings or whole meals of nonperishable foods in the bags and later heat them up easily in a pot of boiling water. The bags can then be used as bowls to eat from, eliminating the need to carry dishes. Another use for these bags is as containers for mixing powdered items such as milk, puddings, eggs, etc., with water. A small spiral wire beater is an invaluable aid for such mixing. ❞❞

---

*"Boilable" plastic bags or "cooking pouches" are available where home heat-sealing devices are sold, such as the kitchen utensil sections of hardware stores. Some grocery stores stock them, and most stock the resealable plastic storage or sandwich bags.

Glenn Porzak
HINDU KUSH SALAD

Bacon (or artificial bacon bits)
Onion (fresh; or reconstituted dry)
Swiss cheese
Cooking oil (or liquid bacon grease)
Vinegar*

Fry bacon, drain off grease, and crumble. Rehydrate dry onion, or chop fresh onion very fine. Chop up cheese into very small pieces. Combine oil and vinegar in desired proportions for dressing. Combine all ingredients.

Glenn Porzak is a lawyer who lives in Boulder, Colorado. He has served as a recent director of the American Alpine Club and for some years has been chairman of the club's Expeditions Committee.

❝ Most of my climbing has been done in the Colorado Rockies, where I have made more than 400 ascents, including the Diamond on Longs Peak and several first ascents. In 1974 I became the first person to have climbed all ninety-eight named peaks over 11,000 feet elevation in Rocky Mountain National Park. I have also climbed extensively in the Swiss and French Alps, and in Alaska.

I have been on overseas expeditions to Noshaq (24,580 feet elevation) and Korpusht-e-Yakhi (18,688 feet) in the Hindu Kush Range of Afghanistan; to Aconcagua (22,834 feet) in Argentina; and Kilimanjaro and Kenya in Africa. I was leader of the 1978 Colorado Himalayan Expedition that attempted 26,760-foot Manaslu in the Gorkha Himalaya of central Nepal, only a few miles from the Tibetan-Chinese frontier.

The one unsatisfied craving often mentioned by climbers on expeditions or other extended mountain trips is salad. It was while I was climbing in the Hindu Kush in 1975 that I came across an Austrian expedition that had solved the problem under conditions where fresh salad greens simply were unavailable. Their Hindu Kush Salad gave the impression of eating a real salad, and it was delicious. ❞

---

*If it is impractical to take vinegar, buy citric acid crystals—sometimes sold as "sour lemon" or "sour salt"—at specialty shops; these taste like fresh lemon juice when dissolved in a small amount of water.

Jay Zane Walley
BACKPACK-GARDENER'S SALAD

1 cup mixed sprouts
Any wild food available, such as
    grains, onion, dock root,
    watercress, etc.
Peanuts (unsprouted)

Sunflower seeds (unsprouted)
Oil
Vinegar
Salt and pepper

Mix sprouts with any wild foods that are appropriate and available. Sprinkle with peanuts and sunflower seeds. Make dressing by combining oil, vinegar, and seasonings; pour over salad. Serves 2.

Jay Zane Walley is a backpacker, climber, and cross-country skier who particularly enjoys the High Sierra and the desert mountains of Nevada.

❝ One of my greatest passions is Nevada's desert ranges. When you penetrate these barren-looking regions by foot or on skis, you find oases with cottonwood trees, watercress—sometimes even wild mustangs. Above 7000 feet, you may have superb trout fishing.

After a week on the trail, you long for the high delight of a fresh salad. With great ease and little expense, you can become a backpack-gardener, growing vegetables right in your pack. All you need is small heavy-duty garbage bags and a supply of untreated seeds available in any grocery or health food store. Mung, adzuki, or other beans, alfalfa seeds, hulled pumpkin or sunflower seeds, peas, wheat, and hulled peanuts are all excellent, as they are high in protein and vitamins.

To start sprouts at home, put ¼ to 1 cup seeds into a wide-mouthed jar. Cover seeds with lukewarm water and soak overnight. Drain. Keep jar on its side in a dark place, or cover with towel or paper bag. Rinse sprouts 2 to 4 times daily with lukewarm water—this keeps them damp and improves flavor. After each rinsing, drain (easy if you cover jar mouth with cheesecloth or piece of nylon stocking). Before the backpack, transfer sprouts to plastic bags (double, to prevent leaks). Keep on top of pack so they won't be crushed and are accessible for rinsing (use tepid canteen water, as cold water retards growth). While hiking, start new sprouts in plastic bags as you go along. You eat the sprouts, seeds and all. When sprouts have reached edible size, keep them cool if possible and they will stay fresh for about a week.

Another good way to prepare sprouts in camp is to use your cooking pot as a 'walking wok.' Heat oil in pot till it bubbles. Drop in ½ cup of rehydrated freeze-dried vegetables. Stir-fry for 2 or 3 minutes. Add a package of reconstituted dehydrated eggs, and scramble till sticky. Add 1 cup sprouts (any type), and cook till done. Season with soy sauce to taste, or with salt and pepper. ❞

With great ease, you can grow vegetables right in your pack.

Chester T. Rice
PENNSYLVANIA DUTCH SALAD

2 ounces dried vegetable mix
¼ bacon bar (¾ ounces)
¼ cup shredded Swiss cheese

½ cup garlic-flavored croutons
⅛ to ¼ cup Hawaiian-style salad
dressing

Rehydrate vegetable mix by covering with cold water and letting it soak for 15 to 20 minutes. Drain. Add remaining ingredients. Serves 2.

Chester T. (Chet) Rice lives in Kentfield, California, near San Francisco. He started backpacking in the mid-1930's with a packbasket in the Adirondacks. He also skied. He is now semiretired from a San Francisco backpacking equipment company. Over the years he has accumulated much information applicable to mountain trails.

❝ When planning food for an outing, first write down the entire menu for the trip, and assemble a shopping list from that. Dehydrated and freeze-dried foods can be supplemented by careful selection of quick-cooking items from your local grocery store. Try to minimize weight and bulk, and to maximize ease of preparation and appetite appeal.

Figure on about two pounds of lightweight dehydrated and freeze-dried food per person per day. The need varies with the individual, but a typical adult diet runs about 3500 calories per day for backpacking. Most dehydrated foods provide around 100 calories per ounce; powdered eggs and margarine provide about 200 calories per ounce.

Remember that cooking time at 8000 feet elevation is about double that at sea level. A one-pot meal for two persons requires a 1- to 1½-quart cooking pot, and for four persons a 2-quart pot. A lightweight frying pan is handy, and for some menus necessary. Cook over a one-burner stove in most places. If you can have a fire, keep it small; and a grill will come in handy.

To make a savory omelet, stir ⅓ cup cold water gradually into 2 ounces (4 tablespoons) dried egg. Add 1 teaspoon dried red or green pepper, 2 teaspoons dry onion, a crushed chicken bouillon cube, and 1 or 2 pinches garlic powder. Soak for 5 to 10 minutes. Fry in 1 tablespoon margarine. ❞

H. Adams Carter
WIND RIVER ICE CREAM

Dry whole milk
Strawberry jam
Corn snow (or any other snow of mixable texture)

Stir milk, jam, and snow together in any amounts or proportions, to the desired flavor and consistency. This makes a delectable dessert or snack

H. Adams (Ad) Carter of Milton, Massachusetts is a mountaineer of long and extensive experience. He climbed his first peak, Mt. Washington in New Hampshire, in 1919, when he was five years old. In 1936 he was a member of the British-American Himalayan Expedition that made the first ascent of 25,645-foot Nanda Devi in Uttar Pradesh in northern India. Forty years later, Ad returned to Nanda Devi as coleader with Willi Unsoeld of an expedition jointly sponsored by the American Alpine Club and the Indian Mountaineering Federation. This expedition made the fifth ascent of Nanda Devi via a new route, the Northwest Face and North Ridge. In the years before, between, and after the Nanda Devi ventures, Ad has led more than a dozen expeditions to the Peruvian Andes and has climbed extensively in numerous other areas, including Alaska. Since 1959, Ad has been editor of *The American Alpine Journal*, published annually by the American Alpine Club.

❝ On my first expedition to Alaska, in 1933, our food was pretty awful. It was far from nourishing, and there was never enough of it (I actually developed a mild case of scurvy toward the end of the trip). One day when we were stormbound in the tent, we decided to pass the time by playing cards—for high stakes! The most valuable thing we could think of was our ration of powdered milk for one day.

We played cards all day, and by evening I had cornered the entire ration of whole milk, sugar, and cocoa for all six of us. I envisioned the best, creamiest cup of cocoa that anyone ever had. While the others watched with their mouths watering, I mixed up the milk and the powdered cocoa. Next I grabbed the pressure-top can in which we kept the sugar and heaped in the sweet stuff. Hot water completed the ambrosial drink. Ecstatic with anticipation, I gulped a mouthful—and spat it right out. One of my companions had carefully emptied out the sugar and put salt in the can instead. ❞

Perishable Main Dishes

"Beans!"

Lloyd and Mary Anderson
FOIL STEW

1 sliced carrot per person
1 sliced or diced potato per person
Onion to taste, chopped
Ground beef, ¼ to ½ pound per person
Salt, pepper, and other seasonings to taste

Place vegetables in center of 12-inch square of foil. Put meat and seasonings on top. Fold sides of foil up and over, then hem the foil across the top to seal well. This is a natural for cooking over a bed of coals when you can have a campfire. (It can also be cooked over a one-burner stove, by placing 1 foil packet at a time over low flame or inside covered cooking pot.) After 25 to 30 minutes' cooking time, remove bundle from heat and unfold foil, which becomes a plate. Be sure to pack out the foil. (Use raw ground beef early on a trip, unless it can be kept frozen or at least cold.)

Lloyd Anderson of Seattle, Washington has climbed 450 peaks since 1929. Nineteen were first ascents, including the South Tower of Howser Spire in the Bugaboos in 1941. Lloyd has climbed in Mexico, Switzerland, Italy, Austria, Norway, and Japan, as well as in Canada and the United States.

In 1934 Lloyd and his wife, Mary, started a now widely known West Coast recreational equipment cooperative. In the early 1930's, climbing gear could hardly be found locally and was expensive. The Andersons had received some tempting equipment catalogues from Europe, so Mary, who could read and write German, sent off orders for climbing gear that Lloyd needed. When Lloyd appeared on trails in the Cascades with his European-bought equipment, friends asked the Andersons to order for them too.

❝❝ So we did. When an order arrived, it was a festive occasion. We would make a celebration of it by inviting our friends in for dinner. Opening the packages was like Christmas. On the advice of one of our friends, we soon established a cooperative. For several years we handled all the orders from our home. Then we moved into a grocery co-op near the Seattle waterfront, where we displayed two shelves of outing equipment among the groceries. Later we joined a nearby co-op gas station. Little by little we expanded and eventually became established on Pike Street in downtown Seattle. By then we weren't catering only to Northwest customers: our mail-order business was thriving, and we were shipping to outdoor people all over the United States, and in Canada, Mexico, and South America. In time we moved to still larger quarters. The business—from which Lloyd retired in 1971—now has retail outlets in several western cities. ❞❞

Chris Bonington
PEACH PANCAKES

2 cups pancake mix (commercial or *homemade*)	1 fresh peach
	Butter or other shortening
Water or milk for batter of desired *consistency*	Natural yogurt (optional)
	Maple syrup (optional)

Prepare batter. Add peeled and thinly sliced peach. Fry pancakes in shortening till both sides are golden brown. Serve rolled up with yogurt, topped with maple syrup (if available). Serves 2.

Christian (Chris) Bonington, who lives in Hesket Newmarket near Wigton in Cumbria, is a rock climber, mountaineer, writer, photographer, and lecturer. Bonington has climbed in the British Isles, Alaska, the Alps, South America, the Himalaya, and elsewhere. His first ascents include 26,041-foot Annapurna II, 25,850-foot Nuptse, and the Central Tower of the Paine Group in Chilean Patagonia. In 1970 Bonington led the expedition that put two men on top of 26,545-foot Annapurna I by the Southwest Face, a new route. In 1972 he headed the group that first attempted the Southwest Face of Everest and in 1975 led the expedition that climbed that face. Books by Bonington include *I Chose to Climb, Annapurna South Face*, and *Everest—The Hard Way*.

❝ Peach Pancakes were a delicacy that my wife, Wendy, and I used to cheer ourselves up with at breakfast one summer when we camped for several weeks near Leysin, Switzerland—most of the time in the rain.

The importance of food on high-mountain expeditions is emphasized by Mike Thompson in his appendix on food in *Annapurna South Face**: 'Food was the consuming passion and obsession of the expedition....The High Altitude rations, due to the rigours of the Face and the effects of altitude, were subjected to a much tougher testing than food at Base Camp....Some items became popular as new ways of cooking them were devised. At first the Christmas Pudding did not get eaten, except by Tom Frost who regularly ate two at a sitting, but Christmas Pudding Boysen—thinly sliced, fried, drenched in whisky and served *en flambante* with cream—was universally appreciated (except by Frost...). Christmas Pudding Bonington—a thin gruel made by stewing the pudding with melted snow, sugar and whisky—was really only appreciated by the inventor, who nevertheless forced it upon anyone unfortunate enough to share his tent....Far from being too exhausted even to light the Primus, we found that the cooking of long and elaborate meals was the main cultural activity of high-altitude life....' ❞

Annapurna South Face by Chris Bonington, copyright 1971 by the Mount Everest Foundation Annapurna South Face Expedition 1970. Used with the permission of McGraw-Hill Book Co.

Mike Colpitts
MOUNTAIN SUSHI

½ cup water
½ cup sugar
½ cup vinegar (white)
1 teaspoon salt
2 cups cooked rice

Condiments to taste (sardines, salmon, sesame seeds, strips of sliced omelet, mushrooms, bacon bits, etc.)
Dried seaweed sheets

At home, combine water, sugar, vinegar, and salt, and bring to boil. Put hot rice into a bowl, and sprinkle the sugar mixture over it. When rice has soaked up the liquid, form into small balls. Sprinkle one or several of the condiments over the top of each ball; use imagination and creativity. Wrap the completed rice balls in seaweed leaves. The rice can also be formed into a large roll to be sliced for serving. Store in refrigerator before trip. On trip, eat cold. When you learn to enjoy Sushi, it tastes better than candy bars on the trail. The seaweed or prepared Sushi itself can be purchased at Japanese shops or in delicatessens. (In choosing condiments, consider the probable weather—fish, for instance, may not keep well in heat.)

Mike Colpitts, M.D. of Seattle, Washington is a climber and snowshoer who particularly enjoys winter cross-country trips in the Cascades. He spent a year in Nepal, living and working at Sir Edmund Hillary's Kunde Hospital for Sherpas at around 14,000 feet elevation in the Everest area.

❝ The Sherpas don't measure distances the way we do—they use time instead of mileage to describe the distance from one point to another. If you were in very good physical condition, you could walk from the hospital to the Everest Base Camp in a day. When I worked there, we had two basic food courses: rice with potatoes on top, and potatoes with rice on top. We had a gourmet cook, but he could never get the ingredients for fancy foods. However, he did have a gourmet cookbook beautifully illustrated in color, and quite often before a meal I would look longingly at those pictures. It showed me how wrapped up in food we Americans are.

For myself, I like to fast on one-day mountain trips. Going without eating for several hours provides an experience to push back my psychological limits. If I should ever find myself stranded without food for a day or more, it wouldn't be impossible for me to survive comfortably. In fact, a few years ago when I was on the way with a friend to climb Mt. Rainier's Liberty Ridge, I discovered at our campsite that I had forgetton my food. I declined my friend's offer to share his and made the climb and descent without eating. I was a little short on energy, but made the climb in good shape. ❞

Robert Currie
BOILED BEEF SALAMI

2 pounds lean ground beef
½ teaspoon pepper
¾ teaspoon mustard seed

¼ teaspoon finely minced garlic
2 tablespoons meat curing and
  preserving salt*

At home, mix all ingredients thoroughly. Divide into 2 rolls and wrap each in foil; twist ends of foil well. Refrigerate rolls for 24 hours. Put rolls in a pot containing sufficient boiling water to cover. Boil for 1 hour. Remove rolls from water, lay on rack, and punch holes in the foil to drain off excess water. Rewrap in new foil. Freeze till ready for use. This salami keeps well for days (but perishability varies with the weather).

Robert Currie, a U.S. Forest Service employee who lives in Cottage Grove, Oregon has backpacked extensively in the Colorado Rockies and in wilderness areas of Arizona. In 1976 he took part in a University of Nebraska Bicentennial Project; seventeen hikers followed the old Oregon Trail along the North Platte. The route, determined from old diaries and other sources, covered 150 miles from Ash Hollow State Historical Park northwesterly to Scotts Bluff National Monument in west-central Nebraska. For some years, Currie was a backcountry ranger with the U.S. Forest Service in Colorado, working in an area that receives heavy recreational use in winter.

❞ A list of winter backpacking ethics can help everyone by minimizing wear and tear on the landscape. These are some of the most important points:

1. Private property. Ask permission of owner before entering.

2. Dogs. Where backcountry travel routes are maintained, leave dogs at home.

3. Sanitation. Use established facilities before hitting the trail. When necessary to relieve yourself, get well away from established travel routes and water. Pack out toilet paper.

4. Hazards. Be aware of hazards such as avalanches, whiteouts, and hypothermia.

5. Camping. Stoves and foam pads have replaced wood fires and bough beds. If a fire is a must, don't strip trees for fuel, and do scatter your ashes.

6. Trash. Pack out everything, even fruit peels.

7. Wildlife. Don't disturb wild animals. Pass quietly or make a detour. Stay out of elk and deer winter areas.

8. Soil damage. In spring, stay on snow or rocks; mountain soils are very fragile during the thaw.

9. Be considerate of other backcountry users. Educate friends in winter ethics. **❞**

---

*A combination of salt and chemical preservatives, sold under various brand names; available from some retail or wholesale butchers or meat packers' suppliers.

Glenn Kelsey
COFFEE CAN STEW

Boneless meat (chopped)
Fat (a little)
Vegetables (carrots, celery, cabbage,
*   turnips, onion, etc.), cut up fine*

Salt to taste
Seasonings to taste
*Concentrated soup stock**
Water (a little)

Use amounts appropriate for meals planned. The main idea is to sear the meat in a little fat, and half-cook it, to preserve it. Seal meat in a 1-pound coffee can with the finely chopped raw vegetables, salt, and seasonings. Tape the can lid on tightly. Keep as cold as possible at home, in pack, and in camp till time for use. Stew will keep for a weekend in summer with care, and longer in winter. In camp at mealtime, remove seal, add soup stock and water (not too much), and cook 30 to 45 minutes over not-too-hot stove or in coals of campfire. Flatten and carry out empty can.

Glenn Kelsey of Silverdale, Washington is active both in mountain climbing and in search and rescue work. He has ascended Mt. McKinley in Alaska and has made climbs in British Columbia, Wyoming, Oregon, Idaho, and Washington. He has climbed 14,410-foot Mt. Rainier more than a dozen times and has made four winter ascents of the peak by different routes, including the first authorized winter ascent. Kelsey also participated in the recently released Mountain Rescue Association film, "Climbing Country," which stresses mountain safety, as did its forerunner, "The Mountains Don't Care" (both films were directed by Jim Lawless).

❝❝ People who don't get out for winter camping and cross-country travel are missing a bet. Such winter activities require good clothing and equipment, as well as a continuous awareness of weather hazards, terrain, ice and snow conditions, etc. It is a challenge to remain dry and comfortable for a safe return, but it's well worth the effort. The rewards are many: in winter you aren't pestered by bugs; there are few other people around; and the slide alder, devil's club, and other underbrush are covered with snow. There are spectacular possibilities for photography. The clue for a successful winter climb is preplanning and caches of supplies. Be ready to go on short notice, watch the weather reports for a weather break—and go! But the backcountry is no place for an inexperienced or ill-prepared hiker in winter or *any* season. ❞❞

---

*Soup stock can be made from water, meat (usually a cheap cut of beef), bones, seasonings, carrots, celery, etc. Simmer, partially covered, for several hours, till the flavor of the solids is all transferred to the water. Strain out solids and discard. Canned broth, bouillon, or consommé can be substituted.

Eric Ryback
SAWTOOTH DIPS

Whole grain rye snack crackers (plain or seasoned)
Cream cheese
1 5-ounce can chicken (turkey or tuna will do)
Strawberry jam (or other flavor)

Spread crackers with cream cheese and chicken. Dip into strawberry jam, and eat.
(Cream cheese does not keep well in hot weather.)

Eric Ryback of Pocatello in southeastern Idaho operates an outdoor business that provides training in mountaineering, backpacking, snowcraft, wilderness camping, kayaking, and similar skills. In 1969, at the age of seventeen Eric hiked the 2000-mile Appalachian Trail from Maine to Georgia in 81 days. A year later he made a solo hike of the Pacific Crest Trail from north to south in 132 days. The year after that he covered the Continental Divide Trail in the Rockies in 140 days. He wrote *The High Adventures of Eric Ryback* and *The Ultimate Journey* about these trail experiences.

❝ I haven't done major hikes since the Rockies. I have been climbing, backpacking, and enjoying the Idaho outdoors. A few years ago a friend, Jerry Dixon, and I decided to make a 250-mile trip through the Idaho Primitive Area. We started at McCall in west-central Idaho, traveled southeastward through the Salmon Mountains, and came out near Stanley. We went in May, before river trips begin and there are other people in the backcountry, so we could see more wildlife. Streams were up, due to melting snow, and we had to use cross-country skis part of the way.

About thirty-five miles from the end of the trip, when I was an hour ahead of Jerry on the trail, I came to Goat Creek. The water was high, but I thought I could ford the steam; so I took off boots, socks, and heavy clothes and lashed them onto the top of my pack, which was already loaded with skis and poles. I got a big stick for support and started across. About halfway over I decided that I couldn't make it, then found I couldn't go back, then lost my balance and was swept downstream. My skis snagged on a submerged log; I was caught, barely able to bob up for air. I made a total commitment to get out alive and somehow got free. I was then swept farther downstream, entangled in my pack. Then the boots lashed on my pack filled with water and were dragging me back. Not wanting to lose the pack, I struggled till the shoestrings finally broke. The boots were lost, but I got to shore—ironically, the same side of the stream I had started out from. When Jerry arrived, we decided to belay across, which we should have done in the first place. I had to hike out the last thirty-five miles in cross-country ski boots and my tennis shoes with holes in them. ❞

Mary Staley
ICICLE CANYON SANDWICHES   .

French rolls
Butter
Lunch meat of choice
Corned beef (cooked at home or canned)
Cheese

At home, slit open rolls. Butter them well. Fill with generous amounts of sandwich meat, corned beef, and cheese. Wrap in aluminum foil. Keep refrigerated or frozen till you leave on trip. Keep as cool as possible during transport. In camp, drop the foil-wrapped bundles on the coals of a campfire if a campfire is permitted. That's the best cooking method, but the sandwiches can also be heated 1 at a time over a pressure stove with the flame turned low. Turn the foil packages occasionally. When the sandwiches are hot, remove bundles from the heat, open foil, and eat. Each sandwich makes a complete meal for 1 person. Serve with water, coffee, or a fruit drink.

Mary Wilson Staley of Quincy, Washington was climbing in the early 1950's with the outing club at Washington State College (now Washington State University) at Pullman. The group made trips to the Cashmere Crags, an extensive rock climbing area of fine granite spires, on the east side of the Cascades in the vicinity of Icicle Creek and its tributaries. The Cashmere Crags were described by Ralph S. Widrig in the 1949 *American Alpine Journal* as "tall, threatening spires that streak skyward like Dantesque flames."

❝ I was the first woman to scale The Lighthouse, a tall isolated tower that had first been climbed in 1948 by Fred Beckey, Pete Schoening, and Widrig. The next year I returned to the Crags with the Cascade Crag Climbers, a Wenatchee-based club, for an ascent of Boxtop, a minaret-type summit on the Mt. Temple ridge. On that peak we were benighted and had a very tasty evening meal of whole wheat snack crackers spread with a mixed glob of peanut butter and honey. Icicle Canyon Sandwiches are among my camping standbys. They have made many a hearty meal for my husband, Gene, and our four children. ❞

Louis Ulrich
BAKED SOYBEANS

3 cups soybeans
8 cups water (2 quarts)
¼ pound salt pork, diced (bacon can be used)
1½ cups fresh onion, diced

¼ cup dark molasses
1 cup beer
1 tablespoon salt
¼ cup brown sugar
1 15-ounce can tomato sauce

At home, cover soybeans with 8 cups water. Soak overnight. Without draining, place beans in a 5-quart baking dish. Add salt pork, onion, molasses, beer, salt, and brown sugar. Bake uncovered in a 300° oven for 3 to 4 hours, until beans are almost tender. Stir in tomato sauce and bake for 2 more hours, or until beans are tender. This amount makes 12 to 16 servings. Cool, and pack into small meal-sized containers for carrying. The beans can be put into "boilable" plastic bags* for easier heating, and to cut down on dirty camp pots. Freeze beans till time for trip. In transit, keep beans frozen or at least cold as long as possible. In camp, heat up for a quick meal.

Louis Ulrich, a longtime resident of Yakima, Washington was born in Switzerland in the early 1900's.

❝ I was born in the state of Schwyz in central Switzerland. I made my first climb in 1918, when friends and I unsuccessfully attempted Kroente—we had bad weather and also got severe sunburns. Later I climbed Rigi, 5908 feet elevation, which lies between Lake Lucerne and Lake of Zug and is now one of the most frequently climbed peaks in the world. I left the dairy farm where my father worked and went to the French part of Switzerland, not far from Zermatt. There was nothing to do there but climb. You looked at mountains day and night, even in your sleep. I climbed everything in sight between 1918 and 1920. It was my climbing baptism. Our equipment included alpenstocks, nailed boots, and Eckenstein ten-point crampons. My most difficult climb in that area was the Weisshorn. 'Difficult' in those days and 'difficult' now are as different as day from night. You have to take the wording in the context of the period in which the climb took place.

In 1931 I came to Yakima via Canada. Very few Yakima people then climbed seriously. One of my best climbs was on Adams, up and down the Rusk Glacier; to this day no one else has descended by that route. In the 1930's I also did several routes on Mt. Stuart, including one first climbed by Lex Maxwell, Joe Werner, and me, known as Ulrich's Couloir. ❞

---

*Available where home heat-sealing devices for plastic bags are sold, e.g., kitchen utensil sections of hardware stores.

PART THREE

Wild Food Feasting

A minimal knowledge of which wild foods are edible, which really good, and which deadly poison may be very useful in case it becomes necessary to "live off the land." However, with the exception of fish and game (if there is enough to subsist on), wild foods are largely for fun and frills in most recreational outdoor pursuits.

Edible plants may range from peculiar to delicious. Their availability varies with region and season. However, at any time—particularly when the supply is scarce—judgment and restraint should be used when harvesting wild plants. Some species reproduce slowly; others have a hard time existing at all under adverse conditions; and even those that are abundant should be left in plentiful supply to give pleasure to others.

Most varmints, perhaps, are less subject to elimination than plants. They are usually difficult to capture and frequently seem to lack taste appeal (though they can be palatable). There may be some that are protected locally or are "off limits" for some reason. And of course, with nonvarmint game, and fish, local laws must be observed.

As climbers, trekkers, and backpackers get farther and farther from their home terrain, they may find it useful to know about some of the standard foods consumed elsewhere. Many such items, with imagination and substitution, can be tried out at home. Measurements for ethnic foods are given in the metric system, if that is the system in use in the countries of origin.

Wild Plants

Doug Benoliel
COOKED STINGING NETTLES

2 to 3 cups boiling water
¼ to ½ cup fresh chopped onion
1 pinch sea salt
3 cups chopped stinging nettles
  (Urtica dioica)

Butter
Fresh lemon or lime juice, or vinegar
Dash of sea salt and black pepper; or of
  lemon-pepper and salt (to taste)

Bring 2 or 3 cups water to boil. Put in the chopped onion and sea salt. Add the chopped nettles (for best results, pick only the top 4 to 6 inches of young spring nettles). Boil the greens till they no longer have their stinging quality, about 5 minutes. Drain off liquid. Serve the hot stinging nettles (now stingless) and onions, topped with butter, several drops of lemon or lime juice or vinegar, sea salt, and other seasonings. This amount serves 2 with greens to accompany an evening meal. (Wearing leather or heavy rubber gloves is advisable while gathering and chopping stinging nettles.)

Doug Benoliel of Kirkland, Washington is a backpacker, botanist, and landscape gardener and contractor. His firm specializes in working with native plants. In the early 1970's he was an instructor at the Lander, Wyoming base of an outdoor leadership school, a nonprofit group that teaches wilderness and conservation skills among other subjects. His book, *Northwest Foraging*, arose from these varied interests.

❝ When hiking, I like to carry nine to twelve different spices and herbs—the longer the trip, the greater the variety desirable. A good dish using a wild mountain food as the principal ingredient is a hearty soup made from the leaves and stems of Spring Beauty (*Claytonia lanceolata*). By taking only one leaf or stem from each plant, no plant is destroyed. To make the soup, put a package of chicken noodle soup mix in a quart of boiling water. Add ¼ cup chopped onion; 1 tablespoon butter; 2 to 3 cups of Spring Beauty leaves and stems; a pinch each of basil, black pepper, lemon-pepper, dried watercress, and oregano; and 2 pinches each of garlic salt, celery salt, and sea salt. Simmer for 10 minutes before serving. ❞

Eugenia Horstman Connally
SCRAMBLED LAMBS QUARTER

Bacon, a lot
Lambs Quarter (Chenopodium album)
Eggs
Salt and pepper

Fry a lot of bacon in a large frying pan until crisp. Remove bacon from pan, drain, and crumble it. Throw a large quantity of Lambs Quarter into the pan with the bacon grease, and gently cook greens till they wilt. Then break a bunch of eggs into the pan, add crumbled bacon, and scramble the whole mixture. It makes a fantastic breakfast.

Eugenia ("GG") Horstman Connally of Washington, D.C. is editor of *National Parks* magazine, a job in which she can combine her interests in art, literature, wildlife, and the out-of-doors.

❝ My favorite tramping ground is Shenandoah National Park in the Blue Ridge Mountains of Virginia—two hours' drive from Washington, D.C. I belong to a group of friends who assemble once a month at someone's home for a wild potluck dinner; at least one ingredient of each dish must be wild. During spring and summer we often go on camping trips where we forage for our dinner. Sometimes we go to a farm whose owner wants us to identify the wild foods growing on his property. In autumn we usually make a trip to Assateague Island National Seashore, which parallels the coast of Maryland and part of Virginia. There we sample crabs, clams, mussels, and oysters. One summer we went on a canoe 'survival' trip on the Shenandoah River with Joe Sottosanti, who runs a river outfitting concern near Luray, Virginia, and who for eight years fed his wife and four children entirely off the land and the river. Scrambled Lambs Quarter is Joe's recipe.

Many other wild plants make tasty eating. Milkweed pods or buds are good. Choose tightly packed, green flower buds, or pods no longer than 1½ inches. Put them in a pot and pour boiling water over them. Boil 1 minute and drain. Repeat a couple of times. Cover the buds or pods with fresh boiling water, and boil for 10 minutes. Season with butter, salt, and pepper. All parts of the naturalized day lily *(Hemerocallis fulva)* are edible. Early spring sprouts are especially good; the inside white part is very tender and can be eaten raw, sliced into salads, or cooked. The green flower buds can be gathered when nearly ready to open, and boiled briefly. The underground tubers, if firm, are good either raw or boiled for 15 minutes. Or, to make Day Lily Soup, sauté 2 cups chopped tubers and spring shoots, and 8 small wild onions (chopped), in butter till tender. Add them to bouillon. ❞

Judith N. Moyer
MUSHROOM ROLL-UPS

Butter as needed
1 cup chopped mushrooms (any edible
    variety that is firm and fleshy)
2 tablespoons minced onion
1 teaspoon minced fresh parsley

Salt and pepper to taste
½ cup sour cream
½ cup bread crumbs (about)
White bread, sliced

(WARNING: Never eat a mushroom without positively identifying it as an edible variety; otherwise, disaster may follow!) To prepare Mushroom Roll-Ups, melt 2 tablespoons butter in a large frying pan over low heat. Add chopped mushrooms, minced onion, parsley, salt, and pepper. Toss and fry until golden brown. Add sour cream and up to ½ cup bread crumbs, depending upon the moisture that needs to be absorbed. Stir until the mixture becomes a thick roux.

Trim the edges off slices of white bread, and roll the slices flat with a rolling pin or similar object such as a jar. Spread a layer of the mushroom roux on ⅓ of a bread slice. Butter the opposite edge of the bread slice. Roll the bread toward the buttered edge, and press down to seal. Repeat for rest of roux. Fry Roll-Ups in butter, turning them gently until they are golden brown. Cut each Roll-Up into thirds, and serve hot.

Judith N. Moyer of Warner, New Hampshire is a cross-country skier in winter and a mushroom hunter and connoisseur in other seasons. She is a free-lance writer and photographer specializing in education and New Hampshire feature stories.

❝I have been mushrooming since 1974 under the aegis of my mushroom mentor, Maxine Kumin (she is currently poetry consultant to the Library of Congress in Washington, D.C.). Maxine and I became horseback riding partners, and while riding through the woods we gathered whatever edible mushrooms we came across. To carry the mushrooms, we started to wear backpacks.

Actually it is easier to find mushrooms while on foot—but horses and their tack once made it possible to harvest the largest cache of oyster mushrooms (genus *Pleurotis*) that I have ever seen. Max and I were in training for a competitive trail ride—without our backpacks. After riding fifteen fast miles in pouring rain, we spotted a clump of oyster mushrooms twenty-five feet above the ground, in the crotch of a rotting elm. The cream-colored trove proved irresistible. Using the stirrup leather, which is like a long belt, I shinnied up the tree, telephone-lineman style, and tossed the mushroooms to the ground. They fell with the bark still caught in their gills; I too landed horizontally with bits of bark woven into my sweater. Max carried home all sixteen pounds of our find in a soggy sweater-wrapped bulge on her pommel. At home, we warmed up with wine, and mushrooms sautéed in butter. Later we made Maxine's Roll-Ups and other delicacies.❞

"It's either Boletus edulis *or* Amanita muscaria."

Hans Fuhrer
WILD HERB TEA MIX

Hips (fruits) of wild roses (Rosa *species)*
Berries of juniper (Juniperus communis*)*
Yarrow (Achillea millefolium*)*
Wild bergamot (beebalm, horsemint) (Monarda fistulosa *var.* menthaefolia*)*
Pineapple weed (Matricaria matricarioides*)*

To make the mix, first collect the herbs and berries during summer and fall. Dry slowly. The rose hips and juniper berries should be squashed before drying. The yarrow leaves and juniper berries are dominant in flavor and should be used in lesser quantities than the other herbs. Seal the dried mix in plastic bags for carrying. In camp, pour boiling water over a portion of the mixed herbs, and steep for 5 to 10 minutes. The brew has an excellent taste. Try it and you will like it.

Hans Fuhrer of Radium Hot Springs, British Columbia was born in Switzerland and immigrated to Canada in 1963. He is a full-time warden with the Canadian National Park Service and serves on the mountain rescue team.

❝ My hobbies are photography, nature study, skiing, and mountaineering. I have climbed in the Alps and have made numerous ascents in the Canadian Rockies. I have led expeditions in the St. Elias Range in the Yukon and in 1975 was leader of the first successful National Park ascent of 19,850-foot Mt. Logan in southwest Yukon Territory.

After a long, strenuous climb or hike, mountain food—no matter how it is prepared—always tastes better to us than the most expensive meal in a luxurious restaurant. There is the feeling that we have earned our food and that the occasion is special. In the wilderness we may be above timberline, on glaciers or high peaks, perhaps with days remaining before we reach our objective. There is always the possibility of atmospheric conditions changing for better or worse. We can survive only if, before a trip, we carefully prepare our equipment and food.

My favorite breakfast during a leisure hike, when I can spend more time cooking, is a Cheese Crust Sandwich. Cut slices of cheese (any type). Put cheese into a frying pan over low heat, and let it melt slowly to a fine soft crust. Take the cheese crust out of the pan, and let it cool off. Soak up cheese fat in the pan with bread, and brown bread gently. Place the cheese crust between the browned bread slices. For the final touch, fry some bacon or ham and combine with the Cheese Crust Sandwich. This can be washed down with coffee or Wild Herb Tea. Good! ❞

Ben Guild
BOILED FIDDLEHEAD FERNS

Young curled fern heads of bracken fern (Pteridium aquilinum)
Salt and pepper
Butter or margarine

Pick the young tender "fiddlehead" fern shoots when they are 1 to 6 inches high. They are at their best when still shaped like fiddleheads. Wash, and remove the brown leaf covering. Boil under tender (½ to 1 hour), and season with salt, pepper, and butter. This makes a good vegetable dish to go with other camp foods. The young fern heads can also be fried in butter or margarine and eaten with toast or crackers. Or they can be eaten raw with salt.

Ben Guild of Eagle River, Alaska is a naturalist. He has written many magazine articles about his experiences in recent years with wild foods and animals, and is the author of *The Alaska Mushroom Hunter's Guide*, the definitive text of Alaskan fungi; and two other books, *The Alaska Psychoactive Mushroom Handbook* and *Home Grown Mushrooms in Alaska (or Anywhere Else) and How to Cook Them*.

❅❅ I am preparing a new field guide dealing with the use of wild foods for outdoor people in Alaska. It will cover plants, leaves, roots, fruits, berries, and mushrooms, all common to Alaska. I spend five or six months a year in the Alaska bush. By using wild foods, including game, I can cut my camp food bills in half and get into pretty good shape doing it.

In 1973 I made the second major exploration in forty-three years of the great Aniakchak Caldera on the Alaska Peninsula. This extremely wild, remote volcanic area is a 'wilderness world within a mountain.' I spent six weeks by myself down inside the six-mile-diameter, 3000-foot-deep caldera. Despite some raging storms with winds of hurricane velocity, I managed to photograph and document this amazing ecological phenomenon. I returned in 1976 and 1977 with a partner and reinforced my data on the area. During a six-week period in 1976-1977, we had an exclusive photographic exhibition on the Aniakchak Caldera at the National Park Service's regional headquarters in Anchorage. I worked closely with the National Park Service because the Aniakchak area had been proposed as a new wilderness national monument. This has been accomplished. The area is now called the Aniakchak Wilderness National Monument. I hope in future years to be taking parties into this wilderness region. ❅❅

Steve Markoskie
OREGON GRAPE SYRUP

Ripe berries of Oregon grape (Mahonia) (Berberis species)
Water, a little
Sugar or honey (to taste)

Combine ingredients. Boil for an hour or so, till of a syrupy consistency. This makes a very tasty pancake syrup.

Steve Markoskie of Chehalis, Washington was formerly an instructor at a United States Air Force survival school. He also has taught outdoor recreation courses at Gonzaga University in Spokane and at Spokane Falls Community College. His classes included wilderness survival, first aid, backpacking, snowshoeing, and river rafting. Steve has climbed and snowshoed in the Rockies, Tetons, and Cascades.

❝ Knowing which wild plants are edible and which are poisonous is a pragmatic approach to outdoor understanding and enjoyment. *Know* the plants you eat. Do not eat unidentified beans, bulbs, fungi (mushrooms), or plants with milky sap or fine hairs. White berries generally contain a poison, while blue or black berries are usually safe to eat; red berries can be either edible or poisonous depending on the variety, so specific berry knowledge is required.

Several general tips about plant selection can be employed to ensure the gatherer the best plants available under the most favorable conditions. Usually springtime or early summer provides the most abundant variety of wild foods. If possible look for plants in cool, shaded, moist areas. Immature plants taste less bitter and are more tender than mature ones—look for small shoots or buds that break crisply.

Recipes can be complex or simple depending on several variables, but generally my favorites are quick and easy. First gather the plants and clean them thoroughly. Cook the wild food just as you do food at home, according to individual tastes. There is no great mystery. Boiling, baking, or steaming are my preferred methods.

Wild foods provide a tasty and nutritious change in an often boring trail menu, and they don't have to be carried. They also can sustain a knowledgeable outdoorsman under most 'normal' and emergency conditions. During one phase of Air Force survival training, our group walked a hundred miles cross-country, living off the land as much as possible. Another instructor and I stoned a grouse. The bird's crop was filled with just-eaten huckleberries. So in true survival fashion we all ate some. A few eyebrows were lifted, but this 'food experience' graphically illustrated more complete 'survival usage.' ❞

Varmints

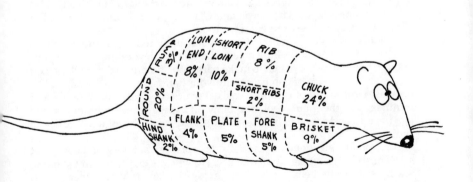

Larry Dean Olsen
MOUSE SOUP

Mouse (or other small rodent, as available)
Wild vegetables
Water

Skin and de-gut the mouse; be careful not to get the blood on your hands (this part isn't easy). Have water nearby to rinse with. Put the mouse in the sun to dry. While it is drying, boil wild vegetables in water. When the mouse meat is half dry, pulverize it, bones and all, to hamburger. Use the Indian grinding method of pounding the meat on a concave or flat rock (a metate) with a smaller hand-held rock (a mano). When mouse is pulverized, add it to the boiling vegetables. The meat should be done in about 10 minutes. You can substitute packrat, woodrat, desert kangaroo rat, woodchuck (lowland marmot), ground squirrel, etc., for mouse.

Larry Dean Olsen is the author of *Outdoor Survival Skills* and for many years, with a trained staff, taught survival techniques in Montana, Utah, and Nevada. Several universities and colleges also offered his courses.

❛❛I learned survival methods on my own when I was growing up around Jerome in southern Idaho. I started teaching professionally in the mid-1960's. Students in such courses often arrive with absolutely no survival knowledge. They learn to live off the land without any utensils or previously manufactured items—with only their bare hands in the desert/ alpine environment of the western United States. But living off the land is pretty much the same worldwide: you learn to use what is there.

Among the edible plants found all over the arid West is biscuitroot (*Cogswellia* or *Lomatium* species) which belongs to the carrot family; it is also called cous or cowish. The Lewis and Clark Expedition called it 'Bread of Cows' and traded horses to get it for food.

Cattail roots make good flour. Carry this or flour from home in a pouch. To make Ash Cakes, scoop a little hole in the flour with your fingers, and pour enough water into the pouch to make part of the flour into dough. Pinch off pieces about the size of golf balls; with your hands, form cakes shaped like tortillas. Drop into hot campfire coals. Turn once. Roast cakes for about 5 minutes, pull them out, cool, and blow off ashes. Spread with butter and jam (if any), and eat. Wild berries can be sealed inside the folded cake before cooking.

Wild plants are generally socially acceptable, but lots of people get squeamish about eating small rodents. However, those who can't stand to see mice and rats being cooked can enjoy the flavor. Mouse meat tastes remarkably good—something like beef.**❜❜**

Barry Prather
JUNEAU ICEFIELD GO-ATTER STEW

1 spotted Go-Atter	*1 carrot (fresh or dried)*
4 glugs water	*1 onion (fresh or dry)*
Dash salt and pepper	*Dehydrated potatoes, to taste*

A Go-Atter is a bushytail packrat or woodrat. (Woodrats are distinguished from house rats by hairy—not scaly—tails. Bushytail woodrats have squirrel-like tails and usually live above the pine belt. The Juneau Icefield Go-Atter is Neotoma cinerea.*) After catching and cleaning the Go-Atter, put 4 glugs of water in the pot—a glug is the sound water makes when poured from a plastic canteen tipped at a 45° angle. Bring water to a boil. Add seasonings, vegetables, and Go-Atter. Boil till the smell drives you out of your tent or snow cave. Then you are ready to eat anything else. Recommended when regular climbing food becomes unpalatable (or scarce). Four field mice can be substituted for 1 Go-Atter. (P.S. The preparer might not want to clean the Go-Atter before using—probably save on seasoning.)*

Barry Prather of Ellensburg, Washington is a geophysicist whose work has included a fifty-three-day stint on top of 14,410-foot Mt. Rainier, twenty summers on the Juneau Icefield in Alaska, three trips to the polar ice north of Alaska, and an austral summer in Antarctica. He is also a climber and was a member of the 1963 Mt. Everest Expedition.

❝ In 1959, when taking part in a project that was seeking a high-elevation site to test astronauts, I planted pinto beans on the side of a steam fumarole on top of Mt. Rainier—it was probably the highest garden ever planted in the contiguous forty-eight states. The seeds germinated in only a week; but when the sprouts were an inch and a half tall, the air temperature frosted them. We tried hot caps over the plants, but the warm vapor steamed them to death.

On the Everest expedition, I assisted Dr. Maynard Miller in geologic research. Subsequently I became an assistant of Dr. Miller's in research being done on the Juneau Icefield. One year we made the unusual discovery that woodrats were living in a nearby nunatak—they didn't turn out to be our favorite form of wildlife. In 1976-1977 I was in Antarctica for the National Science Foundation. The Ross Ice Shelf is 30,000 square miles of perfectly flat terrain, with a continual wind mostly from the south in the austral summer and from the north in winter.

One climbing meal I will never forget is a macaroni-and-cheese dinner I was boiling up in a snow cave. Just as it was ready to eat, I tipped over the stove, the pot flew, and the food spilled out all over our snow bed. I grabbed a nearby shovel, scooped up the mess—and it was quickly eaten, pine needles and all. But thereafter I was relieved of all cooking chores. ❞

Fish and Game

*"Why no, I thought he was a friend of **yours**!"*

Rainer Brocke
STEWED SQUIRREL IN FOIL

1 *squirrel*
Bacon strips

Completely skin and clean squirrel. Cut body of squirrel into 2 portions. Wrap meat with strips of bacon. Wrap meat and bacon in foil; crimp the edges of the foil carefully. Cook until the meat falls off the bones. This should be done in an oven or over a bed of coals, but with care could also be done in a covered pan over a one-burner stove. Game birds such as grouse or pheasant cooked in the same way generally turn out rather well; skin and clean bird, but leave it whole for cooking. Meat prepared by this method goes well with potatoes and a vegetable of one's choice. Recipe serves 1 (but 2 squirrels per person might be required).

Rainer Brocke lives in Long Lake in northeastern New York State. He is a senior research associate coordinator of the Adirondack Wilderness Fauna Program at the State University of New York's Newcomb campus. He has long been an enthusiastic backpacker.

❝ Years ago we used to live on a farm. Each fall I had the opportunity to hunt fox squirrels there; they were quite abundant. When I discovered this recipe, our whole family—including my daughter, who was then three years old—became 'nutty' about squirrels cooked this way. This dish was often served to guests of ours, particularly those who turned up their noses at game. Their expressions of delight had to be seen to be believed. There is a nutlike taste to squirrel meat that is somehow complemented by the smoky flavor of bacon. Also, the bacon fat bastes the meat—game is usually dry—and the foil keeps in the moisture. Two squirrels per person are usually sufficient. The recipe is not original with me, but I have used it many times and can vouch for it. For backpackers and hunters it is tremendous. Rabbit can be substituted for squirrel, but usually is better prepared by other methods.

This recipe is deceptively simple, considering the fantastic results! The end result is hard to match with the most elaborate cuisine. ❞

Sandy Bryson
HALFMOON HIGH TROUT

White flour
Salt, pepper, and herbs garni
Trout
Butter
Almonds, finely chopped

Wild herbs (onion, bay leaves, etc.) if
   available
Dry sherry or sauterne
Wild greens (optional side dish)

At home, premix flour, salt, pepper, and herbs garni. Seal well in plastic sack for carrying. In camp, catch and clean trout. Shake fish in the flour bag. Sauté in pan with butter, almonds, any available wild herbs, and wine. (If the trout outsmart you, substitute a can of smoked salmon.) Serve with wild salad greens such as watercress or wild lettuce, if there are any.

Sandy Bryson of Pacific Grove, California is the founder of a search and rescue dog unit. She has participated in numerous rescue missions, has taught avalanche rescue technique, has worked as a Forest Service wilderness ranger, and with her German shepherd, Hobo, has worked on a canine ranger team in Yosemite National Park. Sandy has written many articles for climbing, outdoor, and search and rescue publications, and is author of the book *Search and Rescue Dog Training*.

❝ We spend so much time backpacking that the food we carry is as important as warm clothing and shelter. In recent years, the quality of freeze-dried food has improved markedly, and on rescue missions I eat a lot of it—plus other space-age material such as gorp, candy, and fast foods. But when skiing or hiking for fun, I prefer to sacrifice light weight for culinary regalement.

A delicious nonwild camp dish is stuffed potatoes. At home, bake 2 to 4 potatoes until skins begin to turn crisp and the insides are tender. Slit skin, and hollow out potatoes without puncturing the casing. Mix potato meat with 1½ cups shredded cooked chicken, 1 cup grated sharp cheddar cheese, ¼ cup chopped shallots, salt, pepper, and ½ cup white wine; stuff back into potato skins, and wrap individually in heavy foil for reheating in campfire embers or over stove. These stuffed potatoes keep indefinitely on cold-weather trips, and for a day or two in warm weather (chill or freeze them before a trip).

My funniest food experience happened on a search where my dog found a lost twelve-year-old girl who had done all the right things to keep from freezing to death overnight. She was hungry after her ordeal. Another handler and I dug into our packs for food. When my partner offered her gorp laced with chocolate candies, she very solemnly refused it. She proceeded to wolf down all my dried apricots and jerky, commenting, 'Candy is bad for you. I really never touch the stuff!' ❞

Ellie Horwitz
SQUIRREL FRICASSEE

2 squirrels	Bacon fat or other shortening
1 cup flour	Water
1 teaspoon salt	1 large onion, diced
½ teaspoon pepper	1 bay leaf

Skin and clean squirrels. Cut small ones into quarters and larger ones into fifths (2 hindquarters, 2 front quarters, and a saddle). Roll meat in combined flour, salt, and pepper. Heat fat in a large cooking pot, and brown the pieces of meat on both sides. When meat is brown, cover with water, add onion and bay leaf, and simmer for about 1½ hours. Check liquid occasionally, and add more water if needed. This amount serves 3 to 4.

Ellie Horwitz of Concord, Massachusetts has held outdoor-related jobs with Lane County in Oregon; with the Massachusetts Audubon Society; with the United States Fish and Wildlife Service; with the Society of American Foresters; and with the Massachusetts Division of Fisheries and Wildlife, as chief of information and education. Among her writings is *Ways of Wildlife*, a beginners' book about wildlife needs and behavior.

❝ I was a woods wanderer throughout all my early years, enjoying a little hunting and fishing and a lot of beautiful scenery. Such wandering provided a restful break from teaching seventh and eighth grades in New York City—and I quickly found out that many students who had serious learning disabilities were willing and able to learn all sorts of things outdoors that they would have found dull indoors. Within a few years I discovered that people would pay me to do just exactly what I had always enjoyed doing—wandering, watching, and sharing what I learned. My rambles, always casual, took me all over New England with some exciting times spent in Oregon, Alaska, and even Florida's Okefenokee Swamp.

A good Venison Stew recipe calls for 1 to 2 pounds of venison chunks; butter; a bay leaf; 2 or 3 juniper berries if available; 1 cup beef stock; 6 or 8 pearl onions; 2 or 3 carrots, cut in strips; 2 or 3 potatoes, diced; salt and pepper to taste; a can of corn if desired; and ¼ cup Burgundy. Carefully trim all fat off meat. Sauté meat lightly in butter, in a large pot. Add bay leaf and juniper berries. Add warmed beef stock (or water). Cover, and let simmer for an hour; occasionally check level of liquid and add a little water if needed. Add vegetables, seasonings, and wine. Simmer for another 30 to 45 minutes, or until vegetables and meat are tender when tested with a fork. ❞

Charlie Norton
DEEP-FRIED TROUT CRISPIES

Small trout, such as Midnight Blues or Square-Tails
Lard or other fat, a soup-can full for deep frying

Eastern trout are different from those in the West. They aren't very big, only 3 or 4 inches long, almost minnow-sized. (Consult the local game laws!) Capture a lot of them. As you catch them, fry them on the spot in deep fat. Don't clean them—the deep frying crisps them. Eat the entire fish—head, tail, everything. Excellent!

Charlie Norton of Saratoga Springs, New York has skied, snowshoed, and backpacked for over twenty-five years. He is a gunsmith by trade, specializing in muzzle-loaders.

❝ My favorite area is here in the Adirondacks. This is great backcountry for hiking, skiing, and snowshoeing. Many people who have only read about New York think of the entire state in terms of New York City. They don't realize that we have a lot of wooded, hilly, rural terrain. Adirondack State Park is big, larger than some of our neighboring states, and is a very beautiful area. I enjoy the nearby mountains year round.

I especially like to go canoeing on the Cold River, a stream that starts nowhere and goes nowhere. There are no nearby roads. It is in the northern part of the Adirondack State Park, in the vicinity of Lake Placid, the site of the 1980 Winter Olympics.

I have some good recipes to use when a campfire is possible. One is for pike. Catch one big enough to clean with an axe, and chop out about 5 pounds. Don't scale it. In summer, stuff the chunk of fish with wild onions and dandelion greens (add butter or other fat because it is a dry fish); or stuff it with an onion dressing. Wrap fish in aluminum foil, and roast it over campfire coals. Allow about 20 minutes per side; turn once. Pull the bundle out of the coals, unwrap, and it should be done.

A good way to cook a duck, if you can get one, is to roast it in clay. Collect a good-sized mound of blue clay from along river or lake. Clean duck, remove insides, and fill cavity with leftover corn bread and an onion stuffing mix. Mound clay over duck on the ground, working clay into feathers until well covered. Build a fire on the mound to get a good bed of hot coals. Let coals burn for some 6 hours. Pull off coals, and split open clay mound with axe. The duck's feathers and skin peel off, and the meat and stuffing remain. Delicious eating. ❞

Stephen C. Porter
BOILED TUKTU

Tuktu (caribou) ribs or thighs
Water to cover
Salt
Mayonnaise (optional)

Boil caribou ribs or thighs with water to cover till tender. This is how the Nunamiut Eskimos of northern Alaska cook caribou. It tastes best with plenty of salt, or even better with mayonnaise.

Stephen C. Porter is a mountaineer and professor of geological sciences at the University of Washington in Seattle. He has traveled to many of the world's most rugged and remote mountain ranges, engaged in research on glacial history. He is also editor of *Quaternary Research*, an international journal.

❝ I have been going into the mountains for more than thirty years, for both climbing and research. In recent years, my travels have been mostly in connection with various research projects involving the glacial history of high mountain areas. These include such places as the Brooks Range in Alaska, the Cascade Range of the Pacific Northwest, the Chilean Andes, the Italian Alps, the Hindu Kush in central Asia, the Himalaya, the mountains of Antarctica, the Southern Alps of New Zealand, and Hawaiian volcanoes.

My work has, of course, often involved me in local recipes and ingredients. Boiled caribou was one of my favorite meat dishes in the central Brooks Range during four summers spent in northern Alaska. Roast caribou is good—but for a tasty change, try boiling it.

Not long ago I was working on the recent glacial history of the southern flank of the Mont Blanc (Monte Bianco) massif in Italy. There the local food and wine were so good that I didn't have to resort to trail cooking. ❞

Mina Lou Taylor
TROUT SOUP

2 or more nice-sized trout
¼ cup freeze-dried corn, or handful of
    dehydrated hashed brown
    potatoes
Dry onions to taste
3.2-ounce package dry milk

3¾ cups cold water
Salt
Pepper
Seasoning salt
Butter or margarine
Diced fried bacon, or bacon bits

Catch and clean trout. Fry. Remove skin and bones, and cut meat into good-sized pieces. While fish is frying, rehydrate corn or potatoes, and onions, and mix up dry milk with water to make about a quart. Heat milk. Add reconstituted vegetables, flavorings, and butter to taste. Simmer until vegetables are tender. Add bacon and fish. Cook until chowder is heated through and flavors are blended. Good with pumpernickel or sesame rolls. Serves 2.

Mina Taylor of Martinez, California is active in backpacking, mountaineering, and conservation.

❝ My mountain ascents include many in the Sierra Nevada: Whitney, Brewer, Banner, Lassen (on skis), Starr King, Cathedral Peak via the southeast buttress, and various rock climbs in Yosemite Valley and Tuolumne Meadows. In the Cascades, I have climbed Mt. Shasta, Mt. Hood, and Mt. St. Helens (prevolcano). I have backpacked in Olympic National Park, along the Washington and Oregon coasts, in the Big Sur area in California, and have also made many backpacks in the High Sierra. I recently completed an Annapurna trek in Nepal.

I have a passion for cooking, outdoors and also indoors, which has led me to organize more than a thousand recipes for easy access. ❞

Adam Ustik
FISH HEAD CHOWDER

Fish heads
Water
Onions (fresh or dry), chopped
Potatoes (fresh or dehydrated),
    chopped
Salt

Seasonings that go well with fish
    (chives, sage, basil, parsley,
    marjoram, thyme, etc., to taste)
Mushrooms, dried or fresh
Butter, 1 gob

Boil fish heads in water till gristle can be removed and discarded. Add onions, potatoes, salt, spices, and mushrooms (use dried mushrooms from the market, unless you know your mushrooms and can pick them fresh). Cook until vegetables are done. Add butter. Serve hot.

Adam Ustik of Victoria, British Columbia is an instructor in the Provincial Emergency Program, British Columbia Ministry of Environment. He deals with outdoor emergencies around the clock. Knowledgeable about his province's backcountry, he is also a backpacker, hunter, fisherman, and skier.

❝I was born in The Pas, Manitoba, a Hudson's Bay Company fur trading post. However, I have lived in British Columbia most of my life. I learned woodsmanship from an old-time trapper. Since the mid-1960's I have been engaged in search and rescue work, have set up training programs, and have been involved in other outdoor work for the government.

An anecdote that comes to mind is one of those 'I should have known better' situations. Some friends and I decided to drive up the Alcan Highway some 450 miles to the north of Dawson Creek, for a hunt in the Mt. Roosevelt area. We trucked all our food and supplies up there and established our camp. Then we left all our supplies at the camp and drove on to scout out our hunting area. We were enjoying our scouting trip and eyeballing what we could see of the proposed backpacking area from the road. Somehow we managed to get the truck stuck in the glacier-fed waters of the Racing River. All we had with us was a blunt axe, a hammer, some long nails, and a long-nosed shovel. Everything else (including our food) was in camp.

We managed to cut some big branches to use to make a fulcrum and lever setup. We would repeatedly pry the axle up and throw rocks and timbers under the wheels for traction. We worked hard for five hours, wading around waist deep in the icy water, before we could finally get the truck out. It was one of those situations where the outdoorsman learns something— in this case, that he should always have the necessities for survival with him, not left behind in camp. ❞

Ethnic Adaptations

Mike Cheney and Purma Topgay Sherpa
SHERPA SOUP

1 litre* water
100 grams** sommer (Sherpa cheese)
Garlic to taste
Some chili
Tomato sauce, small amount

To boiled water add sommer, garlic, chili, and tomato sauce. Boil for 5 minutes. Serves 4. "It is very good for climbing," says the Sherpa cook, "because it makes good feeling for the climbers."

SHYAKPA

Salad oil	1 big spoon flour
¼ kilogram*** onion	Butter
½ kilogram meat	1 litre water
1 kilogram potatoes	Chili, small amount

Put some salad oil in frying pan. As soon as it gets hot, put chopped onion in, and brown it. Add meat. Add potatoes, and cook covered for half an hour. While meat, onion, and potatoes are cooking, make flour gravy. Melt butter in pan, and add flour. Cook mixture till it gets brown; stir as necessary. Add water and chili, and boil for 6 minutes. Add this gravy to the meat and potatoes. Serves 4.

Mike Cheney is British and lives in Kathmandu, Nepal, where he has had twenty years of trekking experience. He is executive director of a trekking service of which Dawa Norbu Sherpa is the founder and chief executive.

❧❧ Our trekking outfit, with headquarters in Kathmandu, is the only cooperative organization in tourism in Nepal that strives for grass-roots involvement of local people in the economic development of their region. We offer tailor-made treks for individuals and groups to all the major trekking areas of Nepal, and also to many regions that are hardly on the trekking map. We played a leading role in the 1975 British expedition that

---

*1 litre = 1.057 quarts, liquid measure
**1 gram = .035 ounces; 100 grams = 3.5 ounces
***1 kilogram = 2.2 pounds

put up the new and difficult Southwest Face route on Everest. We were also organizing agents for the 1976 American Bicentennial Everest Expedition and other major expeditions.

These recipes were provided by Purma Topgay Sherpa, who was head cook for the 1975 British Everest Expedition and is on the staff of our trekking agency. Some of the ingredients are strictly local, necessitating substitutions if the dishes are prepared in other areas. **99**

"Did you say a litre was equal to a **cup** *or a* **quart***?"*

Maynard Miller
TIBETAN TEA

4 or 5 cups water
1 or 2 tablespoons Darjeeling tea
½ teaspoon salt (or less to taste)
1 tablespoon butter
Sugar to taste (optional)

Bring water to boil. Add tea, and steep for 15 minutes without boiling again. Add salt and butter. Add sugar if desired—Tibetans do not use sugar in tea. Drink immediately. Or carry in vacuum bottle, and shake well before drinking. It is a good trail tea, as the salt is beneficial on long trips and the butter provides a lift. Darjeeling is an Indian tea grown in the Himalayan foothills on the southeastern border of Nepal.

Dr. Maynard Miller is dean of the College of Mines at the University of Idaho in Moscow, and the chief of the State of Idaho Bureau of Mines and Geology. He is also president of the Foundation for Glacier and Environmental Research, Pacific Science Center, Seattle, Washington. He is a geologist by profession and the author of over 200 scientific papers, reports, and monographs. Dr. Miller has led or participated in more than fifty research and exploration projects in more than seventy countries. His work has taken him to Alaska, Canada, Greenland, Norway, Switzerland, Cuba, Mexico, Central America, the Peruvian Andes, Argentina, Patagonia, Africa, Saudi Arabia, South Yemen, India, Nepal, Thailand, the Philippines, Japan, and elsewhere. Among these expeditions he led the first American ascent of Mt. St. Elias in Alaska (1946) and was field leader on the Mt. Kennedy and Mt. Hubbard Memorial Mapping Yukon Expeditions (1965). He also was geologist on the American Mount Everest Expedition (1963) and since 1946 has directed the annual summer expeditions of the Juneau Icefield Research Program in Alaska, involving upwards of ninety persons in the field each yea .

❦❦ My two favorite geographic locations in the world are similar. I have an Arctic temperament, and I like a challenging, invigorating climate. One of my favorite places is the Alaska-Yukon-British Columbia border region. This area extends from the coast of Alaska through temperate rain forests in the Coast Mountains, on inland across the continental flank of these ranges. There are arctic conditions at high elevations. In the semiarid interior, nights are cold and days warm with an abundance of sunshine. September is the most memorable month of the year in the interior: Indian summer, flies and mosquitoes are gone, and the aspens are gold. The second region I particularly like is the Fitzroy area in Patagonia. It is very similar to the first; but in the Southern Hemisphere, autumn comes in March. Then instead of aspens turning gold, it's leaves of the Nothofagus tree in glowing crimson.

In various places our expeditions lived off the hinterland. In the Amazon you can eat Amazonian ants fried in oil as part of your meat supply. In Patagonia for months at a time we ate mutton that was first barbecued in sunflower oil, and then eaten by hand with cooked onions and potatoes. At every meal, in southern Patagonia and Chile, we drank maté with the natives. This is a mildly sedative native tea made from the yerba buena plant (*Ilex paraguariensis*) that grows in the jungles of Paraguay. The natives relaxedly sit around the *asado* (barbecue) campfire passing a small gourd filled with hot maté. You sip it through a silver or brass straw known as a *bombilla*. If you don't imbibe when the bowl is passed, it is considered an insult. 99

"Floyd, about the cook that you lined up for this expedition..."

Yvon Chouinard
CHIMI CHURI

1 small handful chopped garlic
½ cup oil
1 handful chopped green onions
1 handful oregano

1 teaspoon red chili peppers
2 tablespoons salt
Red wine vinegar

Combine ingredients. Put them in wine bottles, and top off with red wine vinegar. Make some vertical grooves in the corks so you can make shakers out of the bottles. Chimi Churi will keep for years, and you can keep adding more oil and vinegar as it runs out. It is delicious on meat cooked over a fire, especially wild game.

Yvon Chouinard lives in Ventura, California, where he manufactures climbing equipment of innovative design, including ice axes, crampons, chocks, pitons, boots, and clothing. He also spends part of the year in the Tetons in Wyoming. Yvon is world famous for his difficult rock and ice climbs and is the author of *Climbing Ice*. He has climbed in Yosemite, Canada, Scotland, the Alps, Mexico, Africa, Pakistan, and South America. In 1980 he was with a group that attempted to climb the Northwest Ridge of 24,900-foot Mt. Gongga (formerly Minya Konka) in south-central China.

❝ Chimi Churi is especially recommended for Argentina and Patagonia. One use is with Lamb Carne Asada (barbecued lamb), prepared in this way:
1. Walk out of the mountains starving, to the nearest *estancia* (ranch). Make friends with the gauchos. Kill a lamb and leave skin on fence.
2. Make fire and let it burn down to coals. Spear the whole lamb above the coals, and turn as necessary.
3. Sprinkle with Chimi Churi, frequently.
4. Cut off pieces of lamb as they get done. Smother in Chimi Churi, and eat with loud laughter, using your knife only.
Huevos Rancheros is a good dish anytime—in South America, Asia, Africa, Canada, or Yosemite. Make it this way:
1. Barter for 1 egg per person (cigarettes are excellent for barter, which also reduces your companions' supply). Stir up egg with salt and pepper.
2. Find a local vegetable (zucchini, eggplant, cabbage, tomato, wad of greens, etc.). Chop and sauté in fat with crushed garlic, onions, cheese, and mushrooms. (In the Orient, soak mushrooms overnight.)
3. While vegetables sauté, cut a hot pepper in half. Taste gingerly, and add to the vegetables, a tiny bit at a time until they are properly piquant but tolerable to the timid.
4. Heat more fat in separate skillet, pour in egg, and tilt skillet so egg will spread thin. Cook until jelled but not brown.
5. Flop egg onto plate, spoon in vegetables, and roll up to eat.
6. Repeat until egg and vegetable supplies are exhausted. ❞

John Roskelley
HIMALAYAN CHAPATIS

Atta (whole pastry flour, or finely ground wheat flour or meal, in India)
Water
Strong hands, griddle, and hot coals

Add small quantities of water to an eyeballed amount of atta, depending on how many chapatis you want. Knead dough thoroughly with hands, and add water as needed to make dough similar in consistency to that of bread. Kneading is crucial and must be done thoroughly. Take a small gob of dough, and form it into a ball smaller than a tennis ball. With thumbs on top of the ball and index fingers underneath, rotate wad of dough to form a flat circular cake about the size of the average pancake but much thinner, similar to a crepe. The cake must be still thinner; so holding it between your hands in the clap position, start slapping it back and forth, rotating it as you slap it. The importance of having thin cakes, and their being well kneaded, cannot be overstressed.

Put the cake on a flat griddle that has been preheated on coals. Leave for 10 to 20 seconds, until large bubbles form and the outer layer begins to brown. Then flip it to the other side, and cook for another 10 to 20 seconds. When both sides are done, serve plain or with butter or jam. Plain is most likely, since you wouldn't be eating these if you had anything else.

John Roskelley of Spokane, Washington has climbed extensively in Nepal, Pakistan, India, and elsewhere. His most recent climbs in the Himalaya and Karakoram include 27,825-foot Makalu via the West Ridge, in 1980; 23,440-foot Gaurisankar, and the East Face Direct of 20,000-foot Uli Biaho, in 1979; and 28,250-foot K2 in 1978. Among his ascents in previous years were 26,795-foot Dhaulagiri; 25,645-foot Nanda Devi via the North Ridge, a new route; the Middle Trango Tower, a first ascent; Peak XIX in the Russian Pamirs by a new route; the North Face of the Eiger in Switzerland; and unclimbed Huayna Potosi in Bolivia.

❝ I am no cook. Cheese and salami have been my mainstays. However, through too many of my travels in the East, I have had to survive on the local bread—variously known as Chapatis, Chaapatis, or Chapatty's. I have tried my hand at making these bread cakes, but with a certain lack of success. But in Nepal, Pakistan, and India every child from age three on can make them. So maybe American backpackers could too. ❞

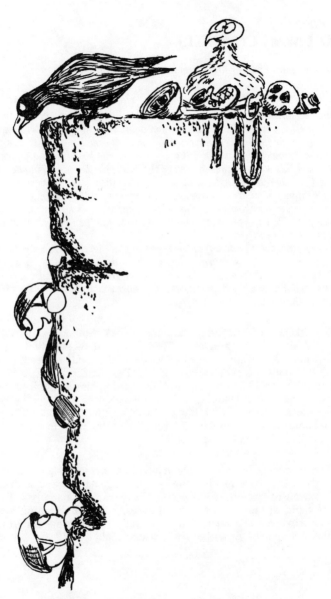

"I'll gather the eggs if you'll cook the omelet."

PART FOUR

Better Food, Less Work

Outdoor menus seem to become simpler and easier as hikes get harder, climbs longer, and the interest in photography, nature study, etc., greater. Apparently there are many ways of eating adequately without wasting much time on cooking.

Outdoorsmen who don't want to cook (but do have to eat) have developed many novel ways of survival. A few outstanding personalities of the good-old-days did it by mooching: a talented young man with only a loaf of bread in his pack could gourmandize for days on samples from his friends' cook pots.

More widely applicable methods (and potentially less hazardous to the health) are described in this section. It must be noted that eating fairly well, while not cooking at all, may require more natural flair than just cooking.

Easier Eating

Fred Beckey
MUSHING ALONG

Fred Beckey, who lives in northern California, started his almost lifetime technical climbing career in 1940 as a young teenager. While he was still in his teens, Fred and his younger brother Helmy made the second ascent, partly by a new route, of the often-tried 13,177-foot Mt. Waddington in British Columbia's Coast Mountains. Since that time Fred has put up innumerable new routes on peaks in the Cascades, Tetons, Wind Rivers, Sawtooths, Beartooths, Wasatch Range, Sierra Nevada, Bighorns, and the southwest desert. He has made ascents in the Yukon, the Bugaboos, and the Coast Mountains in Canada. He has also climbed in Alaska's St. Elias, Fairweather, and Alaska ranges, the Alps, the Nepalese Himalaya, and in Africa, as well as in rock climbing areas such as Yosemite National Park, the Black Hills of South Dakota, and Tahquitz Rock in Southern California.

Fred is particularly well known for his hundreds of ascents, many of them firsts, in the Cascades and is an authority on both the natural history and the human history of that region. His books include *A Climber's Guide to the Cascade and Olympic Mountains of Washington* (1949); the autobiographical *Challenge of the North Cascades* (1969); *Cascade Alpine Guide, Climbing and High Routes, Columbia River to Stevens Pass* (1973); *Cascade Alpine Guide, Climbing and High Routes, Stevens Pass to Rainy Pass* (1977); and *Cascade Alpine Guide, Climbing and High Routes, Rainy Pass to Fraser River* (1981).

❝ I am embarrassed to say that I am probably the worst cook of anyone you know, or may ever know. However, there is one special breakfast cereal that I discovered a few years ago which others might enjoy. It is made only in Canada and is named for a red river—you can't miss it in a Canadian grocery store. It is widely stocked. The grains included are natural whole cracked wheat, rye, and flax. It is by far the best cooked cereal I have ever encountered.

Cook it for breakfast, and serve with butter, brown sugar, and dry milk. Add a few raisins. It is truly excellent. On one trip, a friend who dries his own fruit and vegetables (home style) brought a good deal of his dried fruit along. So we tossed some dried plums, apricots, apples, peaches, etc., into our mush—that made it even better. ❞

John A. Danielsen
RAISON d'EATS

John A. Danielsen, retired, of Flushing, a section of New York City on Long Island, has hiked and backpacked, ski toured and canoed throughout the Catskills and Adirondacks and elsewhere in New York and New England. He has also skate-sailed in various places. He did much work in connection with trails and bikeways in New York State while president of the New York/New Jersey Trail Conference. For three years he planned, organized, and conducted hiking exhibits at the State Travel Center in New York City. He has also conducted orienteering hikes and organized and directed the Conservation Patrol, a volunteer trail patrol in Harriman State Park. He is the author of *Winter Hiking and Camping*, published by the Adirondack Mountain Club, and wrote the article "How to Get Started in Winter Backpacking" for *Backpacker* magazine.

❧ *Winter Hiking and Camping* includes the following advice: 'In a cold climate, food becomes critically important to maintain body temperature, and to provide energy for involuntary body functions and for moving about under varying conditions.... One must be prepared physically and mentally for an extremely high energy output in winter climbing. Food is our only source of energy except for energy stores in the body.... An adequate diet is of critical importance in preventing hypothermia or frostbite....

'For strenuous winter climbing, plan for a daily intake of up to 6000 kilogram calories, depending on the particular conditions encountered .... Food carried should be of the easily digestible, high-energy type.... It should be handy for nibbling—hard candies, dried fruit, fresh fruit (if it can be prevented from freezing), nuts, fruitcake, cheese, hard-boiled eggs. Cheese and hard-boiled eggs spoil on thawing after freezing, so insulate them. Carry a full vacuum bottle of hot coffee, tea, chocolate, gelatin, soup or even sugared water. Chocolate will sour if not used soon enough. Besides their nutritional and warming value, hot drinks are psychological boosters.

'Meals should be of the one-pot variety—glop, mulligan, or hoosh—to be simply and speedily heated or cooked on your stove. Basic ingredients are soup mix, vegetables, rice or potatoes, some kind of meat (...or fish) and seasoning.' ❧

Robert DeWolf
OUTWITTING BEARS

Robert DeWolf of Oakland, California is sales director of a concern that manufactures backpacks and parkas of a high-quality, weather-resistant fabric. His activities include rock climbing, backpacking, and cross-country ski tours. He guides winter outings and gives 'how to' demonstrations for ski touring and winter camping. He has also made a number of long bicycle trips; one was a tour of Maui Island in Hawaii, and others were 500-mile trans-Sierra tours.

❝ On my outings I do not put a lot of time into preparation—to me, food is just something to keep me going outdoors. I plan what I want ahead of time, make a list, and can cruise through a supermarket, health food store, or mountain shop in about fifteen minutes and have what I need for a week's trip. The variety of lightweight instant foods available in a grocery store is amazing. I like to buy individually wrapped foods, such as energy bars and candy in bite-sized pieces. I use freeze-dried foods all year round. In summer I don't take stove or cooking gear. In winter I always carry margarine, salt, pepper, and onion (fresh, dry, or as flavored salt). Onion and margarine are lightweight and inexpensive, and enhance food in winter, especially freeze-dried food which is typically somewhat bland.

A really important aspect of outdoor meals, in areas such as Yosemite, is the technology of hiding food from bears and other animals. It is important to protect both food and equipment—and sometimes yourself. Bears are smart and at least in Yosemite are not afraid of people.

Never leave food inside your tent or pack (or even in unattended pockets). Never leave food near your sleeping bag or let it touch your tent floor or the inside of your pack—just the residual odor will attract bears and other animals. Put your food in one or more waterproof stuff sacks with a drawstring. Hang the cache between two points, away from your equipment, totally up in space. Some people say that ten to fifteen feet off the ground is adequate; I think twenty feet is better. I suspend a lightweight cable between two trees and hang my food high. Bears can chew through a rope but not a cable. If you just hang your sack from a limb, a mother bear knows that the branch won't hold her 400 pounds and will send up her cub. Cubs have learned to climb above a dangling sack, drop, and on the way down grab the cache. But if you hang your sack on a cable between two trees, that can't happen. ❞

John Day
BASIC FOODS

John Day of Medford, Oregon started to climb when he was forty-nine years old. Subsequently he made approximately 200 ascents in the western United States. In May 1960, he was a member of a four-man party that climbed Mt. McKinley. The entire party fell 400 feet on the descent. John broke both legs and an ankle in the fall and spent four days on a glacier at 17,000 feet, in sub-zero temperatures, before being rescued by helicopter. Though he continued to climb after his recovery, his injuries eventually put an end to his climbing career.

John then took up cross-country skiing instead, which at that time was not extensively pursued by American skiers. He traveled to Norway for more information about the sport. On his return, he was asked by the president of the United States Ski Association to direct promotion of cross-country skiing in the United States, work that he pursued for six years. During that period, the popularity of Nordic skiing grew rapidly in the United States. John also participated in various cross-country ski races and was active in the International Ski Federation, an organization that conducts the world ski championships every four years. He attended international cross-country ski congresses in Yugoslavia, Lebanon, and San Francisco.

In the early 1970's, John took up bicycling. In 1977, when he was almost seventy, he set a world record for his age bracket when he rode 403 miles without rest.

❝ My favorite story about food goes back to a 1960 ascent of McKinley. It was a very well-organized trip. We had spares of almost every item of equipment and clothing; and each meal was prepacked for ease and convenience of preparation. But when camp was set up after a rigorous first day, we discovered that eating utensils had been forgotten—there were no knives, forks, or spoons. So we ate with our fingers throughout the climb.

For energy when bike riding, I like to eat hard-boiled eggs, and whole wheat bread spread with peanut butter and jelly. I wash these down with coffee sweetened with honey. I also like a cola drink, defizzed the day before by shaking it and later diluted with one-third water.

I don't recommend exotic foods for outdoor athletes. There is no substitute for good old American meat, potatoes, vegetables, fruits, nuts, and eggs. We used to call those the basic foods. I have consulted American coaches for the Olympic games, and they feel that this type of food suits our energy needs adequately. ❞

Peter Lev and Rod Newcomb
MONO-MENUS

Peter Lev and Rod Newcomb, both of Wilson, Wyoming conduct training courses each January and February for ski patrolmen and cross-country ski tourers in Wyoming, Colorado, and Utah. In the late winter, Peter is a helicopter skiing guide in the Caribou Mountains and the Monashee Range of British Columbia. During the summers, Peter and Rod are instructors and guides in the mountaineering school and guide service that has long operated in the Tetons.

Peter and Rod have climbed extensively in the Tetons and elsewhere. Rod has been on expeditions to Mt. Steele in the St. Elias Range and to Mt. McKinley's east buttress. Peter has been on expeditions to McKinley, Logan, Dhaulagiri, Nanda Devi, Island Peak near Everest, and the Pamirs in the USSR.

&& The idea that you have to take certain foods to eat while climbing is baloney. On McKinley we had the same food for breakfast, lunch, and dinner for fifty consecutive days. For breakfast we had hot whole wheat cereal with milk and sugar. Lunch was invariably green pea soup mix. Dinner was always macaroni and cheese or spaghetti, with two cups of hot chocolate. The only food we didn't get tired of eating after fifty days in a row was macaroni and cheese. We also had some Logan Bread, which is pretty tasty when fresh from the oven, but gets so hard after a couple of weeks that you have to use an ice axe to cut off a piece. But that has its advantages. It lasts longer because you can't eat it very fast.

After the McKinley climb, some of the climbers were stranded in camp because the weather turned bad before they could be picked up by plane. The storm continued, and they had to last out a week with no food. They stayed in their tents and kept as still as possible so they wouldn't burn up any unnecessary energy. When the storm cleared, their friends in Talkeetna had food air-dropped to them, among it a lot of peanut butter in jars. On landing, the jars broke. The climbers were so hungry that they spent the next few days picking glass out of the peanut butter so they could eat it.

A really lightweight food is kasha, grain for a Russian hot cereal (it can be cracked buckwheat, barley, millet, or wheat). A very small amount expands to a huge volume. It is available in health food stores. The brown kasha is better than the yellow. Cook it like whole wheat cereal. Eat with lots of butter or with vegetables and spices. &&

Christine Mackert
FREEZE-DRIED FRILLS

Christine Mackert, M.D. of Portland, Oregon has backpacked and climbed since the early 1970's in the United States, Mexico, and the Alps of France, Germany, Austria, and Switzerland.

❝ I came originally from Idaho and got interested in climbing because I grew up in the shadow of the Tetons on the Idaho side.

In regard to food, ease of preparation is of paramount importance to climbers. Most of my food is freeze-dried stuff, but I have found that it can sometimes be embellished a bit to improve the taste and make it more interesting.

For breakfasts I often take the freeze-dried scrambled eggs that require only the addition of boiling water. Then I add a handful of imitation bacon bits, which can be easily carried in a small plastic container. They add a good flavor to the eggs. This whole breakfast is very light to carry. To doll it up still further, butter an English muffin at home, and bring it along to serve with the eggs.

For lunches, or for emergencies, a couple of dehydrated meat bars can be good as an addition to freeze-dried soups. Such a menu, of course, presupposes that one has a stove for heating water and that one wants to take the time to do so. Anyway, I always have cheese and some carrot sticks along to substitute for hot soup.

My dinners are usually pretty standard fare, freeze-dried meals that I like to dress up with a few spices and herbs. However, for car camps I have a favorite stew that I can make up ahead of time at home. I named it St. Helens Stew, since I always fixed it for car camps before climbing St. Helens (in the days before its May 18, 1980 eruption that blew off the top 1200 feet of the peak). The stew recipe calls for 1½ pounds stew meat, flour, salt, pepper, monosodium glutamate, meat tenderizer, butter, 4 cups water, 1 package instant gravy mix, 2 or 3 sliced potatoes, 2 or 3 sliced carrots, and 2 or 3 pieces celery, diced.

Cut meat in small chunks and roll it in mixture of flour, salt, pepper, monosodium glutamate, and meat tenderizer. Brown thoroughly in butter in frying pan. Put into stew pot. Add water and gravy mix. Stir. Simmer for 1 hour. Add vegetables. Cook until vegetables are tender. Season to taste. This amount serves 5 or 6 people and can be kept for 2 or 3 days if the weather is cool. Reheat as needed. Serve with tossed green salad, rolls and butter—and pie if you have a party of gourmands. ❞

Calvin C. Magnusson
ONE-POT POTENTIALS

Calvin (Cal) Magnusson of Enumclaw, Washington is quality control engineer for outdoor products in a large West Coast outing goods cooperative. Cal has climbed extensively in the Pacific Northwest and in other areas.

⁇ One of my favorite dinners on climbing trips starts out with hot cherry-flavored gelatin dessert with a dash of brandy added. I like to follow that up with a soup made with 3 cans water, 1 package cream of leek soup mix, 1 can roast beef, 1 medium-sized fresh onion, salt and spices to taste, and instant mashed potatoes. Bring water to a boil, and add soup mix. Cut or separate roast beef into small pieces, and add to soup. Add chopped onion and flavorings. Add enough instant potato to make a fairly runny glop (if it comes out too runny, add more potato; if too dry, add more water). The meal is topped off with cooked (not instant) chocolate pudding mix and hot tea. Serves 4.

This meal and other similar ones were first used in 1962 on an outing in the Picket Range of the North Cascades. Two years later, the same menus were served in the Tetons. Because of (or in spite of) the meals, that trip was the beginning of a romance that led to marriage a year later.

Numerous good dinner menus can be assembled by varying the courses. Some of the soup mixes I recommend are beef noodle, green pea, chicken noodle, French onion, cream of mushroom, and vegetable. Excellent main-course combinations include chipped beef and rice; canned ham and instant mashed potatoes; canned chicken and Spanish rice; tuna and noodles; and chopped canned pork and rice. The beverage I serve is usually tea or hot chocolate.

For lunch on weekend trips, one of my standbys is a sandwich made from equal parts of margarine, peanut butter, and honey generously spread on raisin bread. It is high in energy, keeps indefinitely, and is great in any weather. **⁇**

Gerry O'Connor
FRESH FOOD IN THE PACK

Gerry O'Connor operates a guide service based at Eagle River in southeast Alaska. He leads six-day backpacks into remote parts of the state. Working with another guide and a bush pilot, Gerry has taken clients into the Brooks Range, starting at Bettles north of Fairbanks, crossing the continental divide at its northernmost point, and continuing to Anaktuvak Pass. His groups have also walked a section of the original Iditarod Trail in the Rainy Pass area, some 150 miles from Anchorage, and have penetrated the Gold Creek region about fifty miles southwest of Mt. McKinley. Wildlife encountered in these vicinities have included bear, moose, caribou, wolf, fox, and other native animals.

On his own, Gerry has visited many other remote spots in the Alaskan wilderness, among them parts of the Aleutian chain, the Juneau area, and isolated places in the interior. He and his wife, Joyce, have also taken their four young daughters on backpacks of several days' duration.

❝ Most of the people who go on our guide service's treks are from outside Alaska. They bring their personal hiking gear and their cameras. We supply tents, cooking supplies, and food. We don't fix any special foods for our trail trips, but eat pretty standard fare. My method is to bring as much fresh food as possible. I usually provide steak, fresh fruit, and cheese for the first day or two (thereafter I don't have to carry the extra weight).

I also like to take along a fresh salad of cut-up fresh celery, radishes, carrots, onions, and other favorite salad vegetables—but not lettuce or tomatoes, as they spoil too quickly. In the Alaska summers, if you keep the salad stuff out of the sun, it will last for five days to a week. Also the salad vegetables are terrific if added to freeze-dried meals like stew or beans— they really give those dishes some life. ❞

Orra Phelps
THE OLD DAYS

Orra Phelps, M.D. of Wilton, New York was first educated as a geologist and from 1919 to 1921 taught geology at the University of New Hampshire in Durham. In 1927 she graduated from the School of Medicine at Johns Hopkins University in Baltimore, Maryland. Internship, medical practice, and World War II service in the Navy Medical Corps followed.

❝ I received my early outdoor training from my mother, a botanist and naturalist, who took me along on field trips. My outdoor interests spanned many years. On my eightieth birthday I hiked ten miles with a pack, slept in a lean-to, and hiked out next day. But most of my camping, hiking, and backpacking were done in the 1920's and 1930's. I have hiked on portions of the Appalachian, Green Mountain, and Sierra-Pacific trails and covered all of the mileage described in the first *Guide to Adirondack Trails*, which I edited in 1934.

When I started camping in the 1920's, a blanket roll was hung from one shoulder and tied at the hip. Inside the bedroll there might be a can of soup, half a dozen potatoes, and a few carrots. There were no special backpack foods. Everything we took came from the grocery store, or consisted of homegrown products such as garden stuff and eggs. We were fortunate to be able to buy dried soup imported from Switzerland. The dehydrated soup of those days was not a powder put up in foil envelopes as it is nowadays. It came in a round stick about six inches long and an inch or so in diameter. Each stick was cut into six pieces, and each piece made enough soup for one person. We called the result 'dynamite soup.' It was good!

One of our favorite supper dishes was Campstyle Salmon Wiggle. Instead of the standard recipe with peas and salmon in a white sauce, I fixed dried cream of pea soup diluted only enough to make it creamy, heated canned salmon in it, and served it on whole wheat snack crackers (still popular, but at that time a very new product). The same system was used with dried cream of mushroom soup and dried chipped beef.

We developed an ingenious method for transporting eggs (not wanting them in our bedrolls). In a cooking pail, usually carried by hand, we padded the eggs with broken-up shredded wheat biscuits. This precipitated a dilemma when we established camp, usually in an Adirondacks lean-to, because the pail was needed for cooking supper. We put the shredded wheat in a paper bag (there was no plastic then) and the eggs in a safe corner of the lean-to. After supper, shredded wheat and eggs were reestablished in the covered pail, safe from raccoons, until breakfast time. ❞

Wayne Merry
MISHAPS AND MERRYMENT

Wayne Merry lives in the remote village of Atlin, British Columbia where he both writes and runs wilderness treks. He previously spent ten years as a rescue ranger with the National Park Service in the United States and started a mountaineering school in Yosemite National Park. In 1958 with Warren Harding he did the first ascent of The Nose on El Capitan in Yosemite, and in 1972 he led the first ski crossing of the Brooks Range in Alaska.

❝ I am all for simple meals. On long trips I like to eat the same thing every day. For breakfast I like a hot drink made from chocolate-flavored malt beverage mix and instant coffee. Most of my dinners are one-pot affairs with an instant pudding for dessert (except, of course, when leading a paid trek!)

A neglected 'meal' is the so-called Midnight Snack. There's a terrible time, usually about 4 a.m., when you wake up cold and can't get back to sleep. The blood sugar is low, metabolism down, and the night at its coldest. The magic medicine is a good hunk of chocolate. It kicks up your blood sugar, and soon you'll be asleep again, cozy and contented. Just don't tell your dentist.

For emergencies you need some food in the bottom of the pack that is unpalatable enough to remain uneaten till needed. I take a small can (with a cover) to cook in, with packets of parched cornmeal, dried-up raisins as hard as so much gravel, and salty overly dry jerky (also a little can of that lousy commercial pemmican). Parch the cornmeal at home by spreading it thin on a cookie sheet, putting it in a hot oven, and shaking it often till it turns the slightest bit brown. It can be eaten dry washed down with water, or cooked into gruel. If eaten as is, it swells up inside and fills you, so don't overdo it.

One winter in Mount McKinley National Park, three of us went out on a four-day snowshoe trip. In an old patrol cabin with a functional wood stove, I mixed up a huge pan of dried eggs and set the rather liquid batter by the stove, ready for a quick breakfast next day. But in the morning there was something in the batter—one of my oldest felt mukluk insoles that I had hung over the stove to dry. It had been marinating all night. However, no one else had seen this, and as we were a bit short of food I scraped off the excess batter and scrambled the eggs. To explain the flavor, I commented that the eggs were a bit burned.

Later, I wrote one of the guys and told him all. The following Christmas he sent me a bag of 'super trail food' that he said his wife had developed. I was a little suspicious, but it looked like chocolate-covered bridge mix and smelled good; so next day I took the bag along on a climb I was guiding. I offered my client a piece and took one myself. We both bit into it simultaneously—and spat it out. We had each chewed up a chocolate-dipped moose scat. ❞

"You're dipping **what** into chocolate?"

Dianne Roberts
HIGH ALTITUDE SALMON

Dianne Roberts of Seattle, Washington is a backpacker, mountaineer, and mountain photographer. She was expedition photographer on both the 1975 and 1978 American expeditions to 28,250-foot K2 in the Karakoram in Pakistan. Dianne's photographs and mountain articles have appeared in many periodicals, including *National Geographic*. Her husband is Jim Whittaker.

❝ On K2 we found that the food we liked at home was not necessarily what we liked at higher elevations in the mountains. For instance, we found that we had three times more chocolate candy along than we wanted or needed. We had quantities of it left over. We also had thought we would want lots of coffee; but even the most dedicated coffee drinkers found it was not their favorite beverage on the mountain. We preferred other hot beverages such as tea, chocolate, and instant soups.

The most popular food on the expedition was canned fish. We had been supplied with 180 cans of Alaskan salmon. It became the most successful food item on the trip. We ate it for breakfast, lunch, and dinner. I think we liked it because of the oil as well as its nice moist taste. We never tired of it. Sardines, both plain and kippered, were also popular.

Besides the trips to K2, I have climbed in Alberta, British Columbia, and Washington. I grew up in Calgary, Alberta. Once when I was a teenager, a girl friend and I decided to go backpacking for a week in the Banff area. We spent days planning the trip, then packed carefully and drove to the roadhead. As we were about to head off into the mountains with our packs, we found we had forgotten something pretty important—we had come off without any cook pots! Not wanting to give up the trip, we talked it over and thought hard. We finally came up with a successful idea. We removed a hubcap from our VW, packed it with our gear, and found that it doubled admirably for cooking. Innovation and creativity come out of strange situations sometimes and are often successful in the wilderness. ❞

Galen Rowell
HIGH, LOW, AND FANTASY FEASTS

Galen Rowell of Albany, California is an experienced climber who is also a mountain photographer, lecturer, and writer. His books include *The Vertical World of Yosemite*, *In the Throne Room of the Mountain Gods*, *High and Wild: A Mountaineer's World*, and *Many People Come Looking, Looking*. His mountain photographs and articles have appeared in many publications, among them *National Geographic*.

Galen has climbed extensively in North America, New Zealand, and Asia. On a long day in 1978 he climbed with Ned Gillette from 10,000 feet on Mt. McKinley to the 20,320-foot summit, and back down to the 17,300-foot level for a bivouac. In the summer of 1980 he made a ski ascent and descent of 24,757-foot Mustagh Ata in the Pamir Range of western China. It was the first American expedition to climb in China in nearly fifty years.

Over the years, Galen has made over seventy-five new routes, including several difficult rock routes in Yosemite and the first winter ascent of the East Face of 14,240-foot Keeler Needle in the Whitney area. Other firsts he has done include the northwest face of the Great White Throne in Zion National Park in Utah, new routes on Howser and Snowpatch Spires in the Bugaboos of British Columbia, the southeast face of Mt. McKinley, and the 5000-foot granite wall of Mt. Dickey in the McKinley area. He has also climbed in the Southern Alps of New Zealand, was a member of the 1975 American Expedition to K2 in the Karakoram of Pakistan, and climbed the Trango Tower in the Karakoram and 23,410-foot Nun Kun in India's Vale of Kashmir.

❝ I don't have any specific recipes for mountain cooking. I tailor food to the trip. At high altitudes I use freeze-dried foods and improve their taste with the addition of spices. Sometimes I take as many as eight different spices on a long trip—lemon-pepper, garlic salt, dill, black pepper, cayenne, cinnamon, and herb seasonings. For the first night of a low-altitude trip I like to take fresh meat, probably steaks for barbecuing, and maybe fresh melon or other fresh fruits and vegetables.

I have a fantasy that while climbing in one of the mountain ranges of the West, I'd kidnap some farmer's cow. I would tie my backpack on it, hold onto its tail, and have it pull me to a camp in a high alpine meadow, where I would stake it out to graze. Each day after climbing I would milk the cow. Eventually I would slaughter the creature and have all the fresh meat I could eat. ❞

Peggy and Bill Stark
GOURMET TOUCHES

Peggy and Bill Stark live in Leavenworth, Washington, not far from the Alpine Lakes Wilderness Area of the Cascades. There in the 1970's they established a family adventure program to get people into the mountains through instruction in such skills as hiking, climbing, snowshoeing, and ski touring.

❝ Bill and I moved from the East Coast to Seattle in 1941. Starting in 1954, we became more and more active in mountain pursuits. When we retired from our work, we established our family adventure program, first in tents in Icicle Canyon near Leavenworth, later in a chalet. It is a life of continuous outdoor activity, learning, and discovery.

A trick I have discovered that gets a multi-day trip off to a good start is providing each guest, the first night, with a large freeze-dried dinner of the kind that comes in a plastic bowl. Not only is that first dinner easy to fix, but for the rest of the trip each person can use the bowl to eat out of. In addition, we always supply a spoon and cup per person and carry two cooking pots.

I like to spark up freeze-dried dinners. For instance, to Turkey Tetrazzini or Chicken and Rice I add a handful of celery (chopped at home), some almonds for crunch, and a tablespoon or two of sherry for character. To Beef Almondine I add red wine. The wine is easily transported in two-ounce plastic bottles — no one objects to carrying an extra two ounces.

Our dinners aren't all freeze-dried. We have a home food dryer, so can assemble home-dried meals. For one of the most successful, I crumble lean ground beef and cook it in olive oil with a minced garlic clove, chopped onion, and oregano. It is then dried in the food dryer, reconstituted in camp, and seems to make a real hit. Another dish that always impresses our guests is an avocado salad. We carry a ripe avocado in an egg-shaped panty hose container (for an avocado that is too big to fit, I use the large ends of two containers taped together). In a plastic sack we carry alfalfa sprouts. These ingredients are combined with a dressing of oil and vinegar, carried in little bottles.

Those small bottles are useful for many things — salt, pepper, spices, vitamins, etc. I also use one to carry my one mountain cosmetic, a facial oil. On one trip I poured what I thought was my cosmetic oil into my hands and liberally scrubbed my face with it — only to find that I had picked up the wrong bottle and I was well dressed with salad oil and vinegar. ❞

Duncan and Joanne Storlie and Will Steger
WATER AND WINTER RATIONS

Duncan and Joanne Storlie live in Excelsior, Minnesota, just west of Minneapolis. Their partner, Will Steger, lives near Ely, Minnesota, near the Canadian border, on his hand-hewn homestead. Duncan is a river runner and a certified Nordic ski instructor; Will has run 5000 miles of arctic rivers; both are former Outward Bound instructors. Joanne's father, Lou Elliott, in the 1960's founded the American River Touring Association, a nonprofit group dedicated to preserving and protecting wilderness waterways.

The Storlies and Steger conduct a year-round guide service. In summer they lead canoe trips on lakes and down Midwest rivers such as the St. Croix, Flambeau, Root, Kickapoo, Wisconsin, and Mississippi. In winter they lead snowshoe and cross-country ski tours and dog sled trips from a base in Ely.

❝ Our varied summer trips include outings in thirty-four-foot canoes, the type once used by the French-Canadian voyageurs on their fur-trading journeys through the Great Lakes region. These canoes are so large that fourteen to fifteen people have to paddle simultaneously. We schedule one such trip to the uninhabited Apostle Islands on Lake Superior. Another, in the Thunder Bay District of Ontario, follows a hundred-mile stretch of Nipigon Bay on the north coast of Lake Superior. Navigating the Great Lakes is similar to canoeing in the open ocean. Weather dictates our schedule.

On winter trips we travel with skis, dog sleds, or snowshoes. We go into the area north of Ely, among the frozen lakes of the Boundary Waters Canoe Area and along portage trails. We often go out by moonlight. Northern Minnesota is one area left in the 'Lower 48' where the howl of the wolf can still be heard.

Both summer and winter trips are in forested areas where there is an abundance of wood for fuel. Our hearty breakfasts and dinners are often cooked over campfires in enormous Dutch ovens. Particularly in winter we use lots of whole grains. One good quick winter dinner is started at breakfast time. We take a thermos and preheat it. Over the breakfast fire we bring a pot of rice, barley, or millet to a boil. We pour the grain (with the water it was boiled in) into the preheated thermos. It cooks during the day and only needs to be reheated for dinner. However, you can add frozen or freeze-dried vegetables, meat, and seasonings to taste.

Our winter lunches are built around a heavy-duty cookie we call a 'Flap Jack' that contains oil, nuts, oats, etc. Washed down with piping hot tea, the cookies provide the right combination of fast energy and longer released energy to get us over the snow to camp. ❞

Dian Thomas
HOT ROCK

Dian Thomas of Salt Lake City, Utah has been backpacking and cooking outdoors since the late 1950's. She is the author of *Roughing It Easy*, a book which was chosen as a *Field and Stream* book club selection and was translated into several foreign languages. It was followed by *Roughing It Easy 2*. Dian has lectured on outdoor cooking topics in Canada, Mexico, and Japan; has appeared on innumerable television shows in the United States; and teaches a class in "roughing it easy" in the Home Economics Department of Brigham Young University in Provo, Utah.

❝ My favorite hiking and backpacking area is the Wasatch Mountains of northern and central Utah and southeastern Idaho. I originally learned a lot about outdoor cooking on family backpacks. I learned more during the seven years I worked at the Brighton (Utah) girls' camp, first as kitchen aid, then as counselor, and finally as camp director. At Brigham Young University my major was home economics. Later, teaching food classes in a junior high school, I was the first to introduce a unit on outdoor cooking. I now travel a good deal. Among other things, I give week-long demonstrations on the benefits of outdoor cookery to other teachers and anyone else interested.

I have noticed that the current trend in outdoor cooking is for people to do more of the food preparation themselves; they seem to be moving toward more inexpensive methods of provisioning, such as growing and preserving their own fruits and vegetables, making fruit leathers at home, etc.

A useful knack in outdoor pursuits is making do with whatever is available. Did you ever cook your breakfast over a fire, in a paper sack, and eat it from same? Did you ever make your own frying pan out of a forked stick covered with foil? Have you ever cooked dinner on a hot rock?

Here is a good breakfast to cook over the hot coals of a campfire. For each person, you need an orange, an egg, enough muffin batter for 1 muffin (made from a store-bought or homemade mix), and some foil. Cut orange in half crosswise, and scoop fruit out of the 2 halves. Break egg into 1 half of the orange shell. Into the other half pour batter for 1 muffin. Place each orange half on a piece of foil large enough so the edges can be brought to the top and twisted. Place the foil-wrapped orange halves in hot coals for 15 to 20 minutes. While egg and muffin are cooking, eat the meat of the orange. ❞

Willi Unsoeld
LOWER SADDLE SKARDU

The late Willi Unsoeld lived in Olympia, Washington with his wife, Jolene. He was killed in an avalanche on Mt. Rainier, March 4, 1979. Willi started climbing as a boy in 1938. In subsequent years he made numerous ascents in the Cascades, Yosemite, the Tetons, the Selkirks of Canada, and the Alps. He later turned to Himalayan climbing. His early expeditions included attempts on 21,640-foot Nilkanta in India and on 27,825-foot Makalu in Nepal. In 1960 he climbed 25,660-foot Masherbrum in Pakistan. In May 1963, Willi established a new route on Mt. Everest, with Tom Hornbein. They ascended the unclimbed West Ridge and descended via the South Col, making the first traverse of a major Himalayan Peak. Willi was coleader in 1976 of the Indo-American Nanda Devi Expedition that put three men on the 25,645-foot summit via a new route, the Northwest Face and North Ridge. His daughter, Nanda Devi Unsoeld, died of unknown physical causes on that expedition.

During the 1970's Willi taught a variety of programs including outdoor education at the Evergreen State College in Olympia. Earlier he served with the Peace Corps and A.I.D. in Nepal. Subsequent to that he was the executive director of the Outward Bound movement in the United States. During the 1950's he spent seven summers as a climbing guide in Grand Teton National Park in Wyoming.

❝ Lower Saddle Skardu was popular with the Teton guides when I was there. We needed a dish that all clients and guides could contribute to with no preplanning. Ingredients had to be easy to get and to fix. Our solution was to ask each client who signed up for climbing the Grand Teton to bring along one can of soup for dinner at Lower Saddle Camp the first night. When we all reached the Camp, the guide would begin opening the cans—and the clients would ask if we had enough pans. We assured them we had pots for everyone. Then we'd go into a long discussion of how scientific experiments had demonstrated that canned soups were fully miscible in all varieties. When all cans were sitting there opened, we would pour the contents with a flourish into one large pot, stir, heat—and *voilà*: Lower Saddle Skardu.

Somebody always brought dry soup, and derision was rampant as this unauthorized material was tossed carelessly into the pot, plus necessary water and any cans of corn, beans, corned beef hash, and raviolis that might have made their way to the saddle. Initial dismay gradually gave way to appreciation of the full creativity involved. The final gourmet product was served up in the rinsed-out cans (which doubled as cups for the breakfast cocoa). ❞

H. Bradford Washburn, Jr.
CHEMICAL EXPERIMENTS

Bradford Washburn of Belmont, Massachusetts was director of Boston's Museum of Science from 1939 to 1980; recently he retired to work full time for the Museum as chairman of the corporation. Dr. Washburn is a scientist, cartographer, photographer, writer, and pioneer Alaskan climber.

In the 1930's, exploring the Alaska Coast Range, he made early use of radios for intercamp communications and of airdrops to supply advance camps. Later he led an expedition which made the first winter crossing of the St. Elias Range from Canada to Alaska, camping for eighty-four days on ice. Over a period of years he took aerial photographs of thousands of square miles of unmapped peaks and glaciers in the St. Elias Range for the National Geographic Society. His many first ascents in Alaska include Crillon, Lucania, Sanford, Marcus Baker, and Hayes.

In the early 1940's Dr. Washburn was with the United States Army Alaskan Test Expedition that tried out arctic, cold weather, and emergency clothing and equipment. During this period he participated in the third ascent of Mt. McKinley. In 1947 he climbed McKinley a second time with his wife, Barbara, the first woman to climb the peak. In 1951 he was coleader of the expedition that first climbed McKinley by the West Buttress. A fifteen-year period of making field observations and aerial photographs of McKinley resulted in his making the first large-scale map of that mountain.

❝ Our expeditions did not use recipes. Cooking was a sort of chemical experiment. When Jim Gale and I were mapping McKinley, we found that oatmeal was the only trail breakfast we could eat day after day without tiring of it. Foods like this that survive the acid test of repeated use, day after day, are always bland of taste and are not necessarily at all what you'd consider 'delicious' at home. Expedition food should be a judicious mix of things that provide reasonably light weight, palatability, easy preparation, and the qualities of filling you up, sticking to the ribs, and giving you driving power. We used the same old oatmeal, beans, minute rice, stewed prunes, hash, chipped beef, and ham—in all sorts of combinations. If you are spending much time at high elevations, bring a pressure cooker; it greatly broadens the possible variety, saves enormous amounts of fuel, and greatly speeds the meal-preparation process. On long trips, some tiny treats and surprises boost the morale, too!

On one expedition we had unusually good food and were impressed by how good we felt despite the extra weight. I'm convinced that at least half the lack of appetite at high altitude is not at all due to lack of oxygen. It's because you've saved the lightest-weight, easiest-to-carry-and-prepare food to eat up there, and most of this stuff would make you gag if you cooked it beautifully in your own kitchen at sea level!! *Good food*, well prepared, will do more to keep up expedition morale and power than all sorts of psychology and esoteric cuisine! **❞**

Gary Willden
HUCKLEBERRY HAHA'S

Gary Willden of Ogden, Utah has been a rock climber, mountaineer, caver, cross-country skier, backpacker, and river rat since the late 1960's. He has been a backpacking and climbing instructor and guide throughout the West and ran his own wilderness school for several summers. He has explored caves in Utah and surrounding states and has made numerous descents to the bottom of Neff's Cave, one of the deepest known caves in the United States. Gary and his wife, Joan, have five sons. Gary, a member of the faculty at Weber State College in Ogden, conducts classes in physical education and recreation. He is also pursuing doctoral studies in outdoor recreation at the University of Utah at Salt Lake City.

&& For trail meals, I usually settle for a breakfast of instant oatmeal—cinnamon and brown sugar flavor is my favorite. If that's not enough, I add a breakfast tart or bar. Like many outdoor people, I have become pretty much of a traditionalist at lunchtime. I like the predictable but satisfying cheese-crackers-salami-gorp meal. My 'goodie gorp' recipe calls for mixing about equal quantities of chocolate-covered raisins, roasted salted peanuts, small chocolate candies with variegated color coating, and a few cut-up jelly things such as spiced gumdrops.

One of my favorite drinks for evenings around a campfire is spiced apple cider. Several days before a trip I prepare the spice mix. In a bowl, I combine 1 cup brown sugar, ½ pound butter or margarine, and ½ teaspoon each cinnamon, nutmeg, and cloves. I refrigerate this creamy mixture for at least two days. On backpacking trips I put about a teaspoonful of it into a cup of hot cider for each person. I carry the cider in a water bottle. This beverage makes for mellow evenings.

One summer I had a group of clients on a guided backpack in the Wind River Range in Wyoming. That year there was a bumper crop of huckleberries in the Winds. We thought a breakfast of huckleberry pancakes would start the day out right. It took five of us nearly an hour to pick about one-and-a-half cups of the tiny berries. Well, it is nearly impossible to pick the little rounders without also picking some of the equally tiny leaves. We had such a conglomeration of berries and leaves that we almost gave up on pancakes and had breakfast bars instead. Then I hit on the idea of trying to 'pan' the leaves out, much as one pans for gold. Pouring the berries into a shallow pan, I swished them around while blowing gently at the same time. I may have looked like a fool, but we enjoyed our huckleberry pancakes in the end. 99

Simplification Deluxe

*"In the army I **always** cooked my C-rations in my helmet!"*

Colin Fletcher
BARBARIAN'S MENU

Colin Fletcher was born in Wales, was educated in England, farmed in Kenya, and prospected in northern and western Canada. After moving to the United States in 1956 he wrote several books, four of them about his backpacking activities. *The Man Who Walked Through Time* tells of his solo hike through the Grand Canyon of the Colorado. *The Thousand-Mile Summer: In Desert and High Sierra* describes his long walk from Mexico to Canada, in part through Death Valley. *The Complete Walker* goes into detail as to equipment and backpacking know-how. *The New Complete Walker*, written several years later, is a revised version of the earlier book, and considerably longer due to the growing popularity of backpacking and to the evolution of equipment. *The Winds of Mara* tells about his protracted sojourn in a Kenya game reserve.

❮❮ The LIGHTWEIGHT BARBARIAN'S MENU is designed for those with strong motivation and stomachs who for some good or otherwise reason want to reduce both load and cooking chores to rock-bottom minimum.

Dispense with stove, pots, allied paraphernalia. Take one medium-sized can fitted with makeshift wire handle. Also one cup. Cook—i.e., boil small amounts of water, nothing more—in can, suspended by whatever simple system pleases you over very small open fire.

Cornerstone of menu is a meat bar. The great advantage of this rectangular gem, beyond profound stick-to-guttability, is (if you choose the right one) blandness: by adding herbs, dried onions, garlic, etc., you can disguise its faint taste to the point of eating different meals at each squatting. A breakfast variation is a bacon bar—though I for one don't much like its taste.

Breakfast: one meat—or bacon—bar. Lunch: ditto. Dinner: twice ditto.

Crumble bar or bars into cup while water boils. Add zesty flavorings as above or according to fancy. Pour boiling water into cup in sufficient quantity to make soup, stew, gruel, paste or whatever consistency satisfies your urge of the moment. Eat. Mitigate severity of regimen by your notion of perfect trail snacks, rich in carbohydrates, low on stickiness. Meet drinking needs with fruit-type drink mixes and tea (*de rigueur* if you happen to be British-type Barbarian, lightweight or otherwise) or coffee. ❯❯

Paul Frankenstein
SAME THING EVERY DAY

Paul Frankenstein of Seattle, Washington, the winter recreation officer for the Mt. Baker-Snoqualmie National Forest, is a skier, snowshoer, backpacker, and horse packer.

❝ On my mountain trips I try to keep food and its preparation as simple as possible, and as cheap as I can go. I usually make up my own fare from dried foods fixed at home or bought at the supermarket. My meals don't vary much from day to day. Breakfast almost always consists of cooked cereal, whole grain or oatmeal, with raisins, brown sugar, and dry milk. On a long trip I may include a few breakfasts of dried eggs and bacon bits, or hotcakes, or fish if they are biting. Lunch is nearly always salami, cheese, and crackers, and a handful of pemmican for dessert. Dinners are made up of simple ingredients such as instant mashed potatoes, dried vegetables, and one of the cheaper dried meats; sometimes there are fish. On one twelve-day canoe outing in Bowron Lakes Provincial Park in British Columbia, my boy and I subsisted on instant dried meals from the supermarket. They are inexpensive and seem well balanced nutritionally. They combine dehydrated and freeze-dried ingredients, and all you need to do in the way of preparation is to add boiling water.

My most memorable outing was a 1963 pack and saddle trip in the Leavenworth District of Wenatchee National Forest. It was the last trip I made with Slim Hollingsworth, a longtime resident in the Icicle Creek drainage, before he passed away. Slim was a packer, and I served as his helper and cook. The weather at the outset was good, but a strong wind came up at Lake Augusta the first night out and continued to buffet us next morning. Then it began to snow. A mile from Lake Augusta, on a section of trail cut out of a steep slope, a bulky manta pack on one of the horses slipped under its belly. This mishap spooked the stock into a somewhat tangled mass. While Slim controlled the mass as well as he could, I crawled apprehensively between and under horses till I got to the underslung pack. We managed to undo the knots and line up the stock again single file.

The wind and snow continued. After lunch we had a long afternoon ride to Lake Flora, the next campsite. Some of the horses belonging to our guests were tiring. One got so tired that it lay down in the trail, and the rider had to walk the last two miles. The riders drifted into camp as Slim and I built the fire, brewed coffee, and started dinner. We all slept in a big tent except Dale Allen, a woodsman from Lake Wenatchee, who slept under a tarp. Next morning we woke to eight inches of snow on the ground—and were all happy to head out of the high country. ❞

Fritiof Fryxell
STANDARD STORE FOOD

Fritiof M. Fryxell of Rock Island, Illinois was a pioneer climber in the Tetons in the late 1920's and early 1930's. His climbing companions included Phil D. Smith, Robert L.M. Underhill, Kenneth Henderson, Paul Petzoldt, and other early climbers in that area. In part due to Dr. Fryxell's efforts, Grand Teton National Park was established in 1929; Dr. Fryxell served as its first ranger naturalist. Fifty years later, in 1979, he was awarded the Honorary Doctor of Laws degree by the University of Wyoming, in recognition, among other things, of his contributions toward the establishment and development of Grand Teton National Park.

Dr. Fryxell is the author of a number of mountaineering books. *The Teton Peaks and Their Ascents*, published in 1932, served for some years as a climber's guide to the range. *The Tetons, Interpretations of a Mountain Landscape* came out in 1953. His 1978 book, *Mountaineering in the Tetons, the Pioneer Period 1898-1940*, was coauthored with his old climbing partner, Phil D. Smith, who died in November 1979. Dr. Fryxell, as literary executor of the late François E. Matthes, wrote Matthes' biography; his work, through seventeen years, resulted in five books on the Sierra Nevada of California. He is also author of many papers on geology and western history.

&& I came to the Jackson Hole area of Wyoming to do my doctoral dissertation on the glaciation of the Teton Range and Jackson Hole—and wound up climbing all of the major summits by new or difficult routes. Phil Smith and I put registers on the peaks, and, at the request of the National Park Service, suggested most of the place names adopted for Grand Teton National Park.

What kind of food did I carry on the climbs? I ate what I could get at the one store in the area. It was located near Jenny Lake, and it supplied everybody in the north end of the valley. You didn't have to worry about making a choice. You just bought what they had. We used standard canned soups and beans, or candy bars, and I always tried to carry fresh oranges. We made something of a delicacy by putting snow in an orange and eating it. It satisfied our craving for fresh fruit. Sometimes I went without food altogether. **&&**

Vera Komarkova
CANNED, PREPARED, FREEZE-DRIED

Vera Komarkova of Boulder, Colorado, a plant ecologist with the Institute of Arctic and Alpine Research at the University of Colorado, started climbing in the Carpathians in Czechoslovakia, her native country. She has since made many ascents in the Alps, the Rockies, Mexico, Alaska, Yosemite National Park, and in the Himalaya.

She was with an all-woman expedition to Mt. McKinley in 1976 and was one of the two women who, via the South Ridge, completed the ascent. In 1978, as a member of the American Women's Himalayan Expedition, she reached the summit of 26,545-foot Annapurna I with Irene Miller (now Irene Beardsley). In 1980, Vera was leader of an all-woman group attempting the technically difficult Pear Route on the North Face of Dhaulagiri I, a 26,795-foot peak in Nepal. Dhaulagiri was christened "Mountain of Storms" by the Swiss party that first climbed it in 1963.

As a plant ecologist particularly interested in arctic and alpine flora, Vera has spent weeks at a time in camps on the Alaskan tundra and frequently gathers plant specimens during her climbs.

❝ I cook very little when I am climbing. I usually use canned, prepared, or freeze-dried foods. When Tomas Gross and I did a new route on Mt. Dickey in the Alaska Range, we planned on eighteen days of food while climbing a 5000-foot wall. But instead of eighteen days, the climb took twenty-five days. Realizing how slow it was going, we restricted ourselves about halfway up to half rations of food each day. We apparently thought a lot about eating, as we found it difficult to wait the allotted period from one eating time to the next. It seemed particularly hard to wait three hours for a half can of sardines while in our hanging tent. Our food wasn't spectacular—it consisted of instant mashed potatoes, fried luncheon meat, cocoa, orange flavor instant drink, apple cider, dextrose, chocolate, tea with lots of sugar, either dried fruit or meat, and several freeze-dried dinners. The odd thing about it was that we still had one meal left over after we completed our climb. ❞

Arnör Larson
HATE-TO-THINK MENUS

Arnör Larson of Invermere, British Columbia is a technical climber who operates a recreational guide service. His service is unusual in that it caters largely to mountaineers and other outdoorsmen who are already experienced. His program offers outings that include basic and advanced mountaineering; ascents on snow, rock, and ice; and opportunities for climbers to put up new routes. It also features winter recreation such as winter climbing and alpine and Nordic ski touring. His trips take him to the Purcells and the Rocky Mountains of Canada, and range over 15,000 square miles of alpine country, from Golden to Kimberley and from Banff to the Canadian-American border.

❝ I like to take climbers into the wild rugged areas of British Columbia and Alberta, where they can choose and lead first ascents. Sometimes we manage a whole week of first ascents, one each day. I don't like to tie someone on the end of the rope and just let him follow everywhere. I prefer ᵗo have climbers with at least some experience in leading. During the 1970's I guided well over three hundred ascents, including fifty firsts and seventy new routes. During those years we made several new routes on peaks more than 11,000 feet high. The most notable of these was in August 1974, when we made a new route via the West Ridge on 11,150-foot Jumbo Mountain, the second highest summit in the Purcell Range. The best first-ascent year during the 1970's was 1973, when I guided firsts of seven peaks over 10,000 feet elevation. Another new route of interest was made with the late Dr. Leif-Norman Patterson of Golden, British Columbia; we put up a new route on the North Face of 9650-foot Mt. Killarney in December 1971—it was also the first winter ascent of Killarney.

I don't like even thinking about food—let alone packing it. My menus are the *same* every week. I usually just throw in bacon, rolls, bread, jam, honey, peanut butter, macaroni and cheese, potatoes, pudding, hamburger, a canned ham, and whatever else I have at hand. I may be unusual in that I measure my cheese and summer sausage by the centimeter. I can't stand freeze-dried food and don't think it sporting to use it. My worst disasters were forgetting the spoons, etc., and once leaving the whole meat supply in the fridge. ❞

Dick McGowan
BEAR-PROCESSED POUCHES

Richard E. (Dick) McGowan of Albany, California was chief guide at Mount Rainier National Park from 1956 to 1965. He climbed Rainier eighty-three times. He has been a member of eight major expeditions to different parts of the world, including the Everest-Lhotse area in 1955 and Masherbrum in the Karakoram in 1960. He is now in partnership with Leo Le Bon in running a large travel and guide service that schedules trips to various parts of the world, with treks to the Himalaya, China, and other places.

❝ I am a meat-and-potatoes man myself, with a salad and a good dry martini. But that's not the way it always works out, especially on expeditions that require airdrops, etc. The most unlikely food I ever ate was on the 1953 Mt. Logan-Cook Expedition. Four of us—Tom Miller, Tim Kelley, Franz Mohling, and I—spent two months exploring and climbing in the St. Elias Range. In due course we made a first ascent of 13,760-foot Mt. Cook The time came when we had to head out. Hauling a sled, we started out by way of the Seward Glacier, bound for the Malaspina Glacier and the ocean sixty miles away. Rain, fog, and poor visibility made it an uncomfortable trip. Having run out of food, we were anxious to reach our cache at Seward Rock about halfway to the coast. The cache had been stocked with supplies for four days, which supposedly would last till we could reach the beach and another cache.

But when we got to Seward Rock, we found that the five-gallon friction-top tins containing our cached food had provided a field day for a glacier bear. The tins were ripped open; the cans of food were punctured and the contents spoiled; and apparently the bear had swallowed whole the aluminim-foil packets of dehydrated foods and soups. But the bear had—obviously—spent a day or two near the cache. The foil pouches were scattered around in the bear droppings, and apparently the contents were uncontaminated. However, the bear's digestive processes had eliminated labels and instructions. It turned out to be extremely fortunate that we were able to salvage part of that cache, as when we reached the beach a few days later we found that our food cached there had been stolen. The Yakutat beaches are known for the absence of anything edible. But a half-mile stretch contains wild peas that grew after the wreck of the Mara Muru on that spot at the turn of the century. For five days, waiting for clear weather and a pickup by plane, we lived on the food our bear had passed, augmented by fresh peas and pods. ❞

Ray Smutek
HOT BREAKFAST EASY

Ray Smutek of Renton, Washington in 1971 established, and for ten years edited, *Off Belay*, described in its masthead as "The Mountain Magazine, a journal of communication for active climbers and mountaineers." Publication of *Off Belay* was discontinued in 1981. Ray started climbing in 1961 and for some years has run a climbing school in the Cascades which offers a comprehensive program for people with serious mountain interests. The emphasis in his summer courses is on alpine mountaineering, and in winter on avalanche awareness and snow camping.

❝ My cooking skills tend to be limited to boiling water. Also, fundamentally, I am poor. Hence my menu planning involves both a minimum of cooking and a minimum of expensive freeze-dried foods. I can't see much sense in running out to a mountain shop for a weekend's menu. Except for expeditions, which require super-lightweight foods, I buy all my supplies at the supermarket. I occasionally do make use of bulk-packed freeze-dried specialty items which I mix in with ordinary fare.

Breakfast is my particular bugaboo. I like to eat a filling breakfast, but I am also very slow waking up. I have finally worked out a breakfast menu that allows me to turn on the stove and go back and nap while breakfast is cooking. Before starting a trip, I mix together prepared breakfast cereal (preferably of a fairly durable type), dry milk, sugar, and dehydrated fruit. I divide this mixture into individual servings and seal them in plastic sacks. I also buy some sweet rolls, butter them, and wrap them in aluminum foil. I use a good-quality, Swiss-type, nesting double cooker. In the morning, I light the stove. I fill the bottom pot with water and set it over the burner. The top of the cooker, containing the foil-wrapped rolls, is placed over the pot of water (the foil keeps the rolls from sticking to the pot, and no washing is required). When everything is heated up, I pour hot water into the cereal/milk mixture in my cup. When I have eaten that, I make hot chocolate with the rest of the boiling water and drink it with the warm sweet rolls. If there is an easier way to fix a good hot breakfast, let me know. ❞

Jim Whittaker
DRIED OUT DELIGHTS

James W. (Jim) Whittaker of Seattle, Washington was the first American to climb Mt. Everest, in 1963. He was leader of the 1975 American attempt on 28,250-foot K2, the world's second highest peak, and also leader of the 1978 expedition that put four Americans on K2's summit. Whittaker started climbing in 1943 and in subsequent years made numerous ascents in Washington, Alaska, and elsewhere. From 1949 to 1952 he was a guide with the Mt. Rainier guide service, during which period he climbed Rainier sixty-four times. For twenty-four years he was manager of a large West Coast retail and mail order recreational cooperative based in Seattle.

❝I reached the summit of Everest about 1 p.m. on May 1, 1963, with Sherpa Nawang Gombu (a nephew of Tenzing Norgay, who with Sir Edmund Hillary made the first ascent in 1953). Getting the news of our climb to Base Camp was a bit mixed up with food preparation. It was some hours after our ascent before those at Base Camp could be informed. They still had no news from us when, about 5 p.m. on May 1, a radio check was made with Base by the expedition members who were in Kathmandu. The radio contact wasn't wasted, however: the men at Base were struggling over a cooking problem—how to make mayonnaise. The Kathmandu radio operator's wife told them, 'You take some oil and let it drop on an egg very slowly, so the egg will absorb it....' It wasn't until 7:30 p.m. the next day that the problems of poor radio communication were overcome, and news that an American and a Sherpa had reached the summit of Everest was finally relayed to Kathmandu by way of Ceylon. There was so much excitement that those in Kathmandu forgot to ask the men at Base Camp how their mayonnaise turned out.

As far as food and my usual mountain outings go, I don't go to the mountains to eat—I go to climb. So I take lightweight food and use a lot of freeze-dried and dehydrated packaged foods. I just tear open the packages and add hot water. When it's ready, I eat it. Gourmet food in the mountains takes time away from climbing. In 1955, my twin brother, Lou, and I were on a rescue on Mt. St. Helens in Washington's southern Cascades (a popular climb before the 1980 eruption). Lou and I were a day later than expected in getting off the mountain, and we ran low on food. In fact, for our last night's dinner we were down to one slice of bread apiece. We sat there looking at those two pieces of bread, then at each other. It was a meager dinner. We soaked the bread slices in snow—to soften them and add moisture—and ate them. The experience didn't hurt us in any way. We are still climbing. But it did teach us to carry emergency rations at all times.❞

Jim Wickwire
ONE FOOD ONLY

James (Jim) Wickwire, an attorney who lives in Seattle, Washington has been climbing since 1960. His many ascents in the Cascades of Washington include various first ascents. He has made at least eight new routes, or variations of new routes, on Mt.Rainier. One was the first winter ascent of Rainier's Willis Wall via the West Rib in February 1970 with Alex Bertulis. He has also climbed in Oregon, Idaho, British Columbia, Alberta, Alaska, and the Swiss Alps. In Alaska in June 1972 he was with a six-man party that climbed Mt. McKinley alpine style via a new variation on the western rib of the South Face. In 1973, with Dusan Jagersky and Greg Markov, he made new routes and a complete double traverse of 13,560-foot Mt. Quincy Adams and 15,300-foot Mt. Fairweather in southeastern Alaska. The team ascended the complete South Ridge and descended the West Ridge of Quincy Adams, alpine style. They continued the long traverse by climbing Fairweather via the East Ridge and descending the South Ridge.

Wickwire was a member of both the 1975 and the 1978 American expeditions to K2 in the Karakoram. He reached the 28,741-foot summit September 6, 1978, with Louis F. Reichardt; the next day John Roskelley and Rick Ridgeway also completed the ascent. Wickwire remained alone on the summit to take pictures and place microfilmed names of expedition supporters. On the descent he had to bivouac overnight only a few hundred feet from the top. The story of this epic climb is told in Ridgeway's book, *The Last Step*.

❝ I pay very little attention to cooking on mountain trips and always prefer to travel light and to keep it simple. A like-minded climbing friend tells this story on me. He asked what kind of food to get, and I told him to get what he wanted to but to keep it simple and lightweight. He picked up fifty-two instant breakfast mixes—all eggnog flavored. We consumed twenty-four of these per person and climbed Rainier via the Mowich Face on the liquid diet with no problem. We did have some variety, though: we had our instant food hot for breakfast and dinner, and cold for lunch and snacks. Climbers on expeditions develop a craving for spicier foods, such as canned smoked salmon, marinated artichoke hearts, and pickles.

My wife, Mary Lou, prepares an excellent granola mix for my expeditions. She combines the following ingredients: 4 cups quick oatmeal, 2 cups wheat germ, 1 cup coconut, 1 cup walnuts, 1 cup almonds, 1 cup hazel nuts,1 cup sesame seeds, and ¾ cup brown sugar. It is ready to eat on mountain trips, either dry or with added liquid. ❞

Just Not Cooking

"But I thought **you** were going to bring the food!"

Nicholas B. Clinch
LETTING OTHERS DO IT

Nicholas B. (Nick) Clinch of Palo Alto, California is an attorney who started climbing while he was a student at Stanford University. Over the years Nick has made many ascents in California, the Coast Range, the Peruvian Andes, the Himalaya, and elsewhere. Nick has led successful climbing parties in the Karakoram and in the Antarctic.

He was organizer and director of the expedition that in 1958 put two Americans, Peter K. Schoening and Andrew J. Kauffman, II, on top of 26,470-foot Hidden Peak (Gasherbrum I) in the Karakoram of Kashmir. This was the first American ascent of an *Achtausender*—a peak more than 8000 meters high. Nick was also the director of the 1960 American expedition to Masherbrum in Pakistan. The first ascent of this 25,660-foot peak was made by Willi Unsoeld and George I. Bell on July 6, and by Nick Clinch and Captain Jawed Akhter on July 8. Nick was leader of the 1966-1967 American Antarctic Expedition that put up six first ascents in the Sentinel Range. Of these ascents, Nick climbed the 16,860-foot Vinson Massif, 15,750-foot Shinn, and 15,380-foot Gardner in December and January.

Nick was president of the American Alpine Club for three years, 1968-1970, and its treasurer for the following three years. He was instrumental in establishing the Grand Teton Climbers Ranch, which is operated for all climbers by the American Alpine Club under the aegis of the National Park Service. In 1978, the American Alpine Club awarded Nick their Angelo Heilprin Citation for outstanding contributions to the club.

❝ My favorite food is anything that my companions will prepare. I am the world's worst cook. But that's not all bad. It makes for very pleasant expeditions for me. My 1960 trip to Masherbrum was most pleasant from the cooking standpoint. It seems that just before the expedition, Pete Schoening—who had suffered from my endeavors on Hidden Peak in 1958—took Willi Unsoeld to one side and told him, 'No matter how tough it gets, no matter how bad off you think you are, under no circumstances let Nick cook.'

I didn't know this during the expedition. Every time I reached for a stove, my friends would say, 'That's all right, Nick, just go back to sleep; we'll fix dinner. Don't worry about it.' The reason for this unexpected but pleasant deference from my companions didn't become clear till after the trip was over and I found out what Pete had told them. I have always been grateful to Schoening for many things, but his advice to Willi ranks among the top. ❞

Ed Cooper
COLD FOOD

Ed Cooper of Sonoma, California is a nationally known outdoor photographer who made numerous difficult climbs between 1955 and 1962. He pioneered many first ascents and new routes in the Bugaboos of British Columbia, the Cascades, the Tetons, Alaska, and Yosemite National Park. His last Big Wall climb was a new route on El Capitan in Yosemite, the Dihedral Wall, in 1962. Ed's photographs have appeared in magazines such as *National Geographic, National Wildlife, Living Wilderness, Reader's Digest,* and *American Forests*; in Sierra Club publications; in Time-Life books; and in the volume *The Alpine Lakes.* Ed's most recent published major work is a photography book on Seattle. In *Climbing in North America*, Chris Jones described Ed as having "the enviable knack of subsisting on soda crackers and chicken noodle soup."

❝ I recall a four-day trip in the North Cascades when my entire food supply consisted of some hard-type bread, a couple of small cans of meat—and a large plastic bag filled with oatmeal, cornmeal, raisins, dry milk, sugar, wheat germ, and several other ingredients. When I stopped to eat, I put this concoction in a cup, mixed in water, and ate it with a spoon. We bivouacked when night overtook us, without tents or sleeping bags. That was in the early 1960's, but I still do the same sort of thing.

During the years I was involved in technical climbing and going for difficult alpine summits, I had my camera along and took pictures. The images I took became more and more important to me, until my interests shifted gradually to photography. I still enjoy being in the mountains, inspired by beautiful peaks, the flowers, and alpine meadows.

My interest in outdoor cooking might be termed negative—I want to spend as little time on it as possible (I do enjoy fine food—when someone else fixes it). In the mountains I want to maximize the time of wonderment. Cooking and eating subtracts from this, except insofar as it provides fuel for my body to keep going. Most food I take is of a snack nature, to be eaten without any substantial preparation such as cooking. Also, I don't set up camp unless it is absolutely necessary; I prefer to bivouac where I find myself, by choice at a good viewpoint, often on ridges or summits. As a photographer I am busy shooting in daylight hours, especially at sunrise and sunset, the best time for photos. When I am through shooting, there is no time for the usual camping thing. So I take food along that I can eat cold. I don't take a stove, only a spoon, knife, and can opener. Bacon bars, nuts, candy bars, whole grain rye snack crackers, maybe a can of tuna or sardines, cheese, sometimes beef jerky, constitute my diet. ❞

Michael Covington
FASTING AND DYSENTERY

Michael (Mike) Covington is director of a guide service in Alaska and of a guide service and climbing school in Estes Park, Colorado. Mike also conducts expeditions to major mountain areas throughout the world. His climbing accomplishments include many first ascents, new routes, and winter ascents in Yosemite and Rocky Mountain national parks, and elsewhere. In 1975, Mike and Yvon Chouinard made the first direct finish of the Diamond Couloir on Mt. Kenya in East Africa. That same year, Mike, Don Lauria, and Dennis Hennek made the first ascent of 20,423-foot Lobsang Peak on the Baltoro Glacier in Pakistan. On an international expedition in 1977, Mike was with the Italian Reinhold Messner, the Austrian Peter Habeler, and the German Otto Wiedemann on an attempt on the 13,500-foot South Face of Dhaulagiri in Nepal.

❝I grew up in Idylwild in southern California, a few hundred feet below the fine granite of Tahquitz Rock, a prime rock climbing area. This location was an early inspiration, but I didn't fully launch into climbing until moving to Steamboat Springs, Colorado. At the age of fifteen, I departed from a very active life at ski jumping and downhill racing and went fully into climbing.

Based on my experiences in the Himalaya, I offer the following 'recipe' for international travelers:

DYSENTERY ALERT!!

Precautions:

1. Don't eat. This is extremely dangerous and will result in almost certain side effects.

2. Don't drink. Alcohol may be indulged in in small quantities, or as a steroid, but too much may cause dizziness and other weird effects.

3. Don't breathe deeply. This is also extremely dangerous. If possible, attach yourself to an expedition and borrow their oxygen. Don't feel bad about using their air, as they'll be too sick to use it themselves.

Cures:

Even though you pay attention to the precautions, try not to be too upset as you'll probably acquire it in the long run. Therefore, to really get the most out of being abroad, live it up, and enjoy yourself. And when you feel a little rumble in your stomach, just relax, and find a nice comfortable place to sit down. If all this doesn't work, lie down, and pretend you're dying. Perhaps someone will come along and extend a hand in friendship or sympathy. But for the love of God n.ake sure it's the right one—the left may be fatal. ❞

Frank E. Gaebelein
GET-UP-AND-GO

The Reverend Frank E. Gaebelein of Arlington, Virginia made his first climb in 1910, at the age of eleven, when he went up 14,110-foot Pikes Peak in the Front Range of Colorado. Since then he has hiked and climbed in the Cascades, the Tetons, the Wind Rivers, the Colorado and Canadian Rockies, the Interior Ranges of British Columbia, the Sierra Nevada, the mountains of Arizona, and the Swiss and French Alps, and has made ascents in Mexico, England, Scotland, and Iceland. For more than forty years, Dr. Gaebelein was headmaster of Stony Brook School on Long Island, New York. Throughout that time he climbed and wrote articles for various mountaineering journals. He is a free-lance editor and writer.

❝ I am just an ordinary climber who loves the mountains and gets great benefit from mountain outings. I made a few early ascents in the Wind Rivers of Wyoming, but nothing remarkable. In recent years I have pursued the hobby of getting to as many state high points as possible (over forty so far)—I'll never get all fifty, as I am much too old to climb McKinley.

I do not consider myself an outdoor cook. In my climbing and wilderness experiences I have pretty much depended on my companions to prepare our nourishment. On the few occasions when I have climbed big mountains alone, I have carried the simplest of foods. For example, I remember the day in the 1940's when I climbed the Middle Teton. At the saddle between the Middle and South Tetons, an ice-cold wind from Idaho hit me. However, I ate whole wheat snack crackers and canned luncheon meat, and it put new energy in me. When I was climbing with Kenneth Henderson and Casper Cronk in Iceland in 1956, we depended mostly on dried foods. ❞

Peter K. Schoening
ROTTEN BANANAS

Peter K. (Pete) Schoening of Bothell, Washington went on his first mountain outings with the Boy Scouts in the late 1930's. His serious climbing began in 1946-1947. He has climbed extensively in Washington, Oregon, Wyoming, Canada, and Alaska where he made two ascents of Mt. McKinley. He was a member of the historic 1953 American attempt on K2. In 1958, Pete, with Andrew J. Kauffman, II, made a first ascent of 26,470-foot Hidden Peak (Gasherbrum I) in the Karakoram of Kashmir. This was the first American ascent of a peak over 8000 meters high. In 1966-1967 he was a member of the American Antarctic Expedition that made six first ascents in the Sentinel Range. Pete climbed the 16,860-foot Vincent Massif, 15,750-foot Shinn, 15,380-foot Gardner, and 13,620-foot Long Gables. In 1974 the Soviet Sports Federation invited the American Alpine Club to send an expedition to their International Pamir Camp. Pete was leader of the first American party to climb in the Soviet Union (USSR).

❧❧ I do not have much to offer in the way of mountain cooking. You must remember that I date back to the days when food for the weekend was one or two shopping bags of overripe bananas purchased late Friday evening at the public market in Seattle for twenty-five cents a bag. Occasionally we were able to scrounge in someone's kitchen, although this usually occurred only once per climbing partner. As affluence developed, we graduated to ninety seconds through a grocery store, and to one-pot meals instead of a banana weekend.

I was recently invited to go to the mountains with a family group. They were to provide the food. Each meal was a five-course affair or more, with freeze-dried cheese cake for dessert, plates and forks and other eating utensils, etc. There was almost mutiny when I insisted gently that we eat a cold breakfast to get an early start. It was a three-day safari instead of a twenty-four hour ordeal.

Somehow I still yearn for the days when the exhilaration of the climbing and hiking overshadowed the need for food, at least for the weekend. Just put me down for rotten bananas—and oh yes, fresh apples in the fall. ❧❧

William E. Siri
INEPTITUDE AND CHANG

William E. (Will) Siri of El Cerrito, California was deputy leader for the successful 1963 American Mount Everest Expedition. In 1957 he was field leader for an International Expedition to Antarctica. In the early 1950's he went several times to the Cordillera Blanca in Peru, as a participant in high altitude physiological research, and as a member and leader of various climbing groups. Will has made many first ascents and other climbs in Yosemite, the Sierra Nevada, the Rocky Mountains, the Coast Range of British Columbia, the Alps, the Himalaya, and New Zealand. He also filmed "Man in the Antarctic," "Conquest in the Andes," and "Makalu."

Will was a longtime director, and president for two years, of the Sierra Club and served for many years on its Mountaineering Committee. He has been active in various other conservation and environmental organizations.

❝ I was immensely pleased by your request for my favorite recipe. No one has ever asked me before. And despite many mountaineering ventures here and abroad, my companions always seem reluctant to let me cook, although I believe I have an unusual flair for this occupation. I can only attribute this to the human propensity for perpetrating cruel and groundless rumors. After all, who has not melted a pot while heating water. And everyone knows that cooking packaged foods can only produce a substance that has the color and consistency of mud, and that can be rendered eatable only by adding large quantities of chili pepper.

However, since you asked, I do have a favorite recipe that I would like to pass on to future climbers. I call it Approach March Malaise.

1. Pour 1½ ounces of a high-quality Scotch whisky into a Sierra Club cup. Add water to taste. If in the Himalaya, substitute 1 pint local chang, filtered through a nylon sock. Use unwashed sock to preserve flavor and aroma of chang.

2. Bury 2 medium-sized potatoes in hot coals of campfire. Bake for 45 minutes, or until charred layer is at least ½ inch thick.

3. Repeat Step 1.

4. Salt 1 pound beef steak, and drop into fire. In Himalaya, substitute goat or water buffalo.

5. Repeat Step 1.

6. Retrieve steak (beef, goat, or w.b.) and potatoes. *Note*: Do not use ice axe, burning varnish imparts odd taste to steak.

7. Repeat Step 1 while potatoes cool below a red glow.

8. Crack potatoes with a stone, and salt. *Note*: Potato charcoal may be beneficial, possibly necessary, after step 7. Serves one—right. ❞

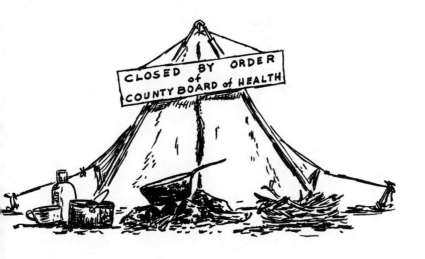

INDEX

About the authors:

YVONNE PRATER has been outdooring most of her adult life, whether hiking and snowshoeing in the Cascades, Rockies and White mountains or helping with the work on the family's farm near Ellensburg, Wash. And, while out exploring, Yvonne has made a profitable habit of taking photographs and compiling information for the illustrated articles she's had published in *Sunset, National Parks* and numerous other outdoor magazines. A writer-photographer for the Ellensburg *Record* for over 22 years, Yvonne also regularly contributes photographs to the *Seattle Times* and other area newspapers. She is the author of the book *Snoqualmie Pass: From Indian Trail to Interstate*, a regional history also published by The Mountaineers.

RUTH DYAR MENDENHALL has happily combined mountaineering, rock climbing, skiing, fishing, backpacking and outdoor cookery for more than three decades, in wild parts of the western United States, and Canada and elsewhere. Her experiences have resulted in articles in *Summit, Desert, National Parks* and other outdoor magazines, and she was editor of the American Alpine Club's *News* for several years. Ruth's culinary expertise was given wide exposure in her two previous books, *Backpack Cookery* and *Backpack Techniques*; she is also the author, with her husband, John, of *Introduction to Rock and Mountain Climbing* and *Beginner's Guide to Rock and Mountain Climbing*.